My QUESTIONS

—

God's QUESTIONS

My QUESTIONS
–
God's QUESTIONS

Brother Ramon SSF

First published in Great Britain in 1998 by
SPCK, Holy Trinity Church
Marylebone Road
London NW1 4DU

British Library Cataloguing-in-Publication Data
A catalogue record of this book is available from the British Library

ISBN 0-281-05142-9

Typeset by Pioneer Associates, Perthshire
Printed in Great Britain by
The Cromwell Press, Trowbridge, Wiltshire

For
My Three Wise Men
Canon A. M. (Donald) Allchin
Brother Anselm SSF
Brother Damian SSF
who may not concur with all the responses
found in this book, but whose constant
fellowship and encouragement have strengthened
my vocation.

Contents

PART THREE **Questions of Practice**

CONTENTS

The God Who Questions

I went to the desert wanting to put a number of questions to God. The idea that God is a retailer of replies dies hard indeed. As a matter of fact, God did not even give me a chance to dig the questions out of my pocket. And, also as a matter of fact, I returned from the desert with many more questions. But they were God's questions. What then of my questions? They had been discarded. I don't even remember them now.

You do not go to God with a platform for speeches or an agenda for discussion. It simply is not possible to channel a conversation with God the way you would like. God goes off at a tangent. He corners you by bringing out into the open the real questions which you have been studiously avoiding.

Thus God turns the tables on you. Now he asks the questions and you have to provide the answers.

(Alessandro Pronzato, *Meditations on the Sand*)

Introduction

A QUESTING FAITH

On a university campus wall someone had painted in large black letters, 'Christ is the answer'. Underneath, in smaller scrawl and with gentle irony, someone else had written, 'What is the question?'

That sums up much of the overt and sometimes aggressive evangelism of some Christians, answering questions which the world has never asked and using language and doctrine which seem to bear no relevance to either the sufferings or the joys of our humanity.

This project began with the sending out of the Questionnaire, reproduced after this Introduction. This was the result of continual feedback I was receiving from my books and from the people who wrote to me, and who came to my hermitage. The various levels of their beliefs and lifestyles often overlapped with the human, spiritual and ecological concerns of many other people who were not Christians – and they had many questions to ask. So I prepared and sent out the Questionnaire, which sets the agenda for the rest of the book.

It may not be the kind of book you were expecting when you picked it up. I hope the words of Alessandro Pronzato (reproduced on the previous page) will halt you in your tracks and turn some of your questions on their head. His words provide our title *My Questions – God's Questions*. These questions, and my prayerful response to them, have involved me in my own journey and have had a similar effect to that felt by Alessandro.

Over the years people have brought all kinds of questions, and sometimes their very lives have become a question-mark. Some of these questions concern the breaking up of their lives, the betrayal of a loving relationship, the painful death of a loved one after months of waiting, watching and praying – and I have felt some of the pain and tears of the questioners.

There have also been the perennial questions of human viciousness and cruelty, the infliction of torture, the suffering and inhuman deprivation in which are manifested the powers of darkness. I do not want to lessen human responsibility for massacres and concentration-camp evil in Bosnia, Rwanda, Burundi and elsewhere, but there are dark, malignant powers at work which are not explained merely as massive psychic forces of evil. They are more personal and objective than that.

Sometimes, in the face of such tremendous evil, I have pointed to the New Testament witness to the powers of darkness which militate against divine love. For while the conflict continues there seems to be no meaning or solution to the agonized questioning. But what I have also tried to do, while I cannot 'answer', is to place my arms around the sufferer and respond with some sharing in sympathy and common compassion. Too often suffering people have been handed dogmatic or intellectual answers to the problems of human frailty, finitude and suffering. Such answers have only satisfied academic theologians, and have served to turn people away from the compassionate God who alone is able to sustain and save them in such distress.

In this book my aim is somewhat simpler and more modest. My method has been extended over some 18 months. I have taken the questions, mulling over them in my periods of prayer and meditation, during my digging and garden work, in my thinking periods and sometimes in conversation with the limited number of friars and people I see each month. Then I have taken them into my hut chapel and laid them before the Lord, much as Hezekiah did with the threatening letter he received from the heathen king Sennacherib (2 Kings 19.14–19). His letter raised all sorts of fearful questions, not to do with doctrines or theories, but attacking the very existence of Hezekiah and the people of God. God was his only refuge – there was nowhere else to go.

Then one cannot be flippant in questioning God. You can be angry, joyful, serious, yearning – or at the end of your tether. But not matey, arrogant or scholastic! What I did not set out to do was respond in a simplistic or glib manner. God is not an omniscient answering machine (and neither am I), at which you 'pays your money and presses the button' so that an answering light flashes on with an instant solution.

Rather I have taken the questions seriously, compassionately, prayer-fully, joyfully, reasonably and sometimes humorously, letting the light of God's Spirit shine upon them, so that my response is the filtering of his light through my mind and heart. Thus it is possible to be prophetic without being arrogant, dogmatic or bad-tempered; to be compassionate without being soft, sentimental or vague.

As you work through the book you may find what Alessandro found – that these questions are transformed under prayerful consideration. Indeed, it may be that they are not answered in the expected manner, but become the basis for further thought and prayer. We shall then find that we are confronted with our true selves before God, and are being questioned and scrutinized by the divine love, and that love both illu-minates and burns!

I do not profess to have novel or original light upon the basic and harrowing perennial questions of faith and doubt, but as a believing and teaching Christian I do have a particular vantage-point of solitude, sim-plicity and prayer which is vitally relevant in a world in which we are caught up in the frenetic consumerist values of money, power, ambition and military might. Profit and self-affirmation are in the air we breathe, and the violent power-games which surround us are often called 'the real world' in which we are obliged to participate.

My vantage-point indicates an alternative view and lifestyle, and an invitation to gospel values which begin at the level of the personal, and have implications for social and political action. I do not want to make too much of this, for my simple lifestyle and enthusiastic faith is just my way of believing in and following Jesus – the way I live out our common baptismal promises. It is modest and small in its way, but it is also revolutionary in its questioning of the ambitious postures and structures of dogmatism and violence in the Church and in the world.

I write as a ecumenical Christian. I do not mean by that term a free-lance, independent spirit who finds no Church pure or holy enough in life or doctrine. I mean a Christian who has put roots down in a particular tradition (Anglican in my case), but who is open to all other Christians who name Jesus as Lord, and to all other human beings whose minds and hearts are set upon compassion and love.

The questions in this book have come from (in alphabetical order) Anglicans, Baptists, Brethren, Catholics, house church members, Methodists, Orthodox, Pentecostals, Presbyterians, Quakers, Salvation

Army members and non-Christians. I am saddened at the divisions in the Church, but I have many dear friends of different denominations, and the communion of our love and fellowship in Christ proves stronger than our denominational differences.

Neither honest believers within the Church or sensible people in the world will put up with denominational quarrels and shibboleths. If we continue to project a distorted image of tribal religion instead of the warm and dynamic love of Christ, then may our churches empty, the walls fall down, the spires collapse and the organs fall to pieces!

We must plant our roots deep down into a biblical and sacramental faith in Christ; we must listen to the fathers and mothers of the Church, and share openly with our sisters and brothers in the faith. Then the diverse communions within the Church of God will be felt to be part of the unity and common vision, and we shall experience the unity of the Spirit in the bond of peace, 'until all of us come to the unity of the faith and of the knowledge of the Son of God, to maturity, to the measure of the full stature of Christ' (Ephesians 4.3, 13).

So read Alessandro Pronzato's quotation again, then read through the following Questionnaire, and begin the journey of question and response with me. Perhaps 'my question' will become 'God's question', and that will be the starting-point of a new and powerful pilgrimage for the reader, and for

Ramon SSF
The Society of St Francis

The Questionnaire

The following Questionnaire was sent out over a period of 18 months, and over 300 questions and comments were received. There was a lot of repetition and overlapping, so some of the questions reproduced in the book may incorporate more than one original. Permission has been given where names are used, though sometimes alternative names have been used to protect the questioner. The use of the term 'non-believer' is purely descriptive and not judgemental – sincerity and integrity are assumed.

Dear AB,
You are among the friends I pray for regularly, and who regularly pray for me. You know that although I continue to explore the hermit life, much of my time is given to people in prayer, counsel, correspondence and in writing books. During the time you and I have been in touch we have glimpsed something of the joy and sadness of our humanity, and been moved by the compassion of God.

Since my childhood I have been moved profoundly by the Holy Spirit (Judges 13.25), and my whole life has been suffused with meaning, alive with joy, yet also tinged with sadness. This is why I have always wanted to share with people I love some of the insights, experiences and beliefs that have constantly renewed my life with creativity and hope. Such communication has brought me close to people intellectually, intuitively and emotionally, and made me love them more.

Since exploring the hermit life over the last years, none of my enthusiasm for theology or for people has lessened – the reverse is the case. Because you are one of these people, I want you to accept an invitation to share with me a little more in seeking God with an open heart. I wrote a paragraph last week in formulating my approach which is brief and concise enough to show you what is in my mind. Here it is:

> I wonder if you have some 'basic questions' which you would like to put to me (anonymously if you like), which come from deep down in your heart (emotional/intuitional) or your mind (intellectual), and which you would like answered, not glibly, but from a place of compassion and prayer? If so, would you write them out and send them to me? I hope to assemble up to 100 such questions with simple (but not simplistic) comments and response. This venture would then be published so that others can share the fruits of our adventure in seeking for truth in love. I suggest three questions. The first on Christian doctrine, the second on spirituality and the life of prayer and the third on practical matters (ethics, morality, lifestyle).

Since writing the above, a fourth question suggests itself from my own experience. I have always had some non-Christian friends, among whom are some I love and respect deeply. Sometimes we have had humorous hot debates, and sometimes clear disagreements. But often I have felt nearer to some of them than to my 'believing' friends. The questions they have asked have often been profound and basic, yet simple and to the point. Your fourth question may come from such a person in your own life – or perhaps from the unbelieving part of yourself.

Use whatever layout you want, but it would be easier for me if you had some kind of method in stating the questions – even if you need to enlarge upon them in a covering letter. I shall not only bring my mind to bear upon the questions, but also make them a matter of meditation and prayer, so that you and I together can expect the wisdom of God to mingle with our endeavour (James 1.5). . .

May I ask if you are willing to have a go in response to this invitation? Let me know, and then you can take what time you need in formulating the questions.

I look forward to hearing from you, and remember you in prayer,

In the joy and peace of Christ,

Brother Ramon SSF

PART ONE

Questions of Belief

1

Is Christianity the Only Way?

Q *Jesus said: 'I am the way, and the truth and the life. No one comes to the Father except through me' (John 14.6). There are many good people who are not Christians, and there are many holy and godly people of other faiths. Is Christianity really the only way? (Simon)*

R This question has appeared in many forms, Simon, and I've chosen your way of asking it. I know that you are wholly committed to Christ, but I have also felt your exasperation, bordering on impatience, when you have been confronted by the exclusivism of some Christians. Perhaps I can respond to your question in this way: 'No, Christianity is not the only way, but Christ is!' By that statement I want to make a distinction between the cosmic Christ or Logos, and the historical Jesus – a distinction grounded in the New Testament itself.

The cosmic Christ is the eternal Word, or Logos, which was with the Father and the Holy Spirit from all eternity (John 1.1). At Bethlehem, he became incarnate in the historical Jesus, and that is what the Christmas carol means:

> He came down to earth from heaven
> Who is God, and Lord of all.[1]

or again:

> Veiled in flesh the Godhead see,
> Hail the incarnate Deity![2]

At certain points in John's Gospel, Jesus refers to himself as the pre-incarnate Logos, such as in the words: 'Before Abraham was, I am' (John 8.58). He was here speaking of himself as the eternal Logos who dwelt with the Father before the foundation of the world, and not simply as the human Jesus who was born of Mary.

If we link the words in your question to this understanding of who Jesus was, we may say that all those who 'come to the Father', of whatever colour, class or creed, actually come through the eternal Logos, whether in creation or redemption. Therefore, those among the saintly people of Judaism and other world faiths are not excluded. Not everyone who is in the kingdom belongs to the Church, for the kingdom is wider than the Church. There are many of Christ's sheep who are not 'of this fold', but those also he will bring into the 'one flock' with one shepherd (John 10.16).

Let me restate it, for it is important both theologically and in forming a positive and inclusive attitude to all religious people in any culture. The eternal Logos became incarnate in Jesus. But as the Logos, together with the Father and the Spirit, Jesus is creator, sustainer and redeemer, enlightening everyone who comes into the world (John 1.9).

The good news of the gospel is that the Word made flesh in Jesus became the Saviour of the world, and that his death and resurrection are the means of the world's salvation. All those who confess and receive him become members of his Body, the Church, and of the fold which is part of the larger flock and the larger kingdom.

Abraham, Isaac and Jacob, and all the Old Testament believers, are in the kingdom, though not part of the Church. Among these are Simeon and Anna in the Temple, the repentant thief on the cross and the great John the Baptist. None of these belong to the post-Easter Church, but they are all part of the kingdom of God.

Because Christ is the cosmic Saviour and Lord, he also shines in all that is true, good and beautiful in the world, and enlightens all those whose hearts are turned towards love and towards God, in all religions and none.

It must also be said that there are many professing Christians who adhere to the institutional Church (clergy among them) who do not belong to the Church which is the mystical Body of Christ – neither do they have a part in the kingdom. Dante places bishops and popes in hell! Indeed, some of the most wicked people have been religious, and some of the most terrible movements inspired by the devil have been fanatically religious – such as crusades, holy wars and *jihads*. Religion

4

may be a passport to hell rather than a door to heaven. That is why I repeat that *no* religion is preferable to bad religion.

In short, all those whose hearts are set on God, whose lives manifest healing, love and reconciliation, are on the path of the divine love, and though they may not be within the Church, they are among the saved, and shall be found in the kingdom of God.

Reflection
We desire to share the love of the Lord Jesus with all those we meet, but to be delivered from an exclusive and bigoted spirit. We desire to discern the light of the cosmic Christ in all that is true, good and holy, and so enlarge our horizons of the kingdom of God.

2
Being Born Again

Q *Is it possible to be a Christian without being born again? (Martin)*

R This is no academic question for you, Martin, for I know that your concern is with your relationship with God, and you tell me in your covering letter that when people ask you such a question, your reply is that you have always been with the Lord, and he with you, and you are perplexed that people seem to want a day, a time and a place of your conversion! The whole matter is complicated by the fact that there is a feeling at large among ordinary, intelligent people, that 'born again' Christians are of a certain intrusive and fundamentalist type, and that they can be threatening and even belligerent in their approach to others, though this may sometimes be a defensive tactic.

I have no intention of allowing one section of the Christian community to monopolize such a beautiful biblical concept and bring it into disrepute. I am born again, and so are my Catholic and Evangelical friends who are open, loving, warm and compassionate in their Christian profession.

5

Some years ago I was the speaker at a conference for Religious in Belfast, consisting mainly of Roman Catholic monks and nuns, but also with a sprinkling of Church of Ireland and Presbyterian folk. During the lunch break, a nun who could not have been five feet tall, said to me: 'Brother Ramon, here in Belfast I am sometimes approached by people who ask me, often fiercely, "Are you born again?" and I don't know how to answer them, for I don't quite know what they mean.'

I replied: 'Sister, answer me one question: do you love the Lord Jesus?' 'Oh, I do', she said with a warm smile upon her face. 'Well, next time someone tries to evangelize you in that manner, look them straight in the eye and say confidently, "Alleluia!" and see what their reaction will be.' We talked a little about the meaning of the term, and I should like to have been a fly on the wall when the next intrusive evangelist tackled her!

You see, that little nun wasn't used to going around telling all and sundry that she was born again, but she did confess Jesus as her Saviour and Lord, though in the context of a believing community. This indicates that the new birth is not an individualistic matter, though it is intensely personal. It is a new birth into the family of God, into the Body of Christ. And it is not simply *my* repentance or *my* faith – indeed, it's not anything that I can do, for the powers of the new birth refer to the whole movement of God in the human heart, in the believing community and in the world at large. The powers of the new birth are cosmic as well as personal.

The occasion when Jesus speaks of being born again (really born from above) is during his night conversation with Nicodemus (John 3.5–8), and the only other time the term is used in this way is in 1 Peter 1.23, where the new birth is associated with the word of God.

The concept of regeneration is more frequently found (Titus 3.5), though this is usually associated with cosmic renewal and restoration (see Matthew 19.28 and Acts 3.21).

The powers of the new birth are clearly cosmic according to Romans 8, where Paul speaks of believers, together with the whole of the yearning creation, groaning in labour pains until the whole cosmos is redeemed, and we are clothed in immortality. So to make the new birth a matter of an individual decision at conversion is to limit its scope and not to appreciate its depth.

The powers of the new birth are not to be confined to a decision at an emotional evangelistic rally, nor to an external religious rite, but are to be seen in the context of the Spirit's re-creation of fallen human nature within the redemption of the whole created order. This will not be consummated until the second coming of Christ in glory.

You can trace the (re)generating power of the Holy Spirit among the people of God from the story of God breathing his Spirit into Adam (Genesis 1.7), through to the prophetic promise of a new heart and a new spirit for Israel (Ezekiel 11.19; 36.26-8) – a promise that the whole nation would know the regeneration pictured in the vision of the valley of dry bones (Ezekiel 37.1-14).

The promise of a new heart and a new spirit is strongly present in the Old Testament, but its fullness is seen in the coming of the Holy Spirit on the day of Pentecost (Acts 2.1-13), which fulfilled what Christ had accomplished in his redemption, for the renewal and regeneration of a fallen humanity into the new Israel, the Church which is his body.

Anyone who wants to do a real study of this can get hold of a dictionary of theology, and look up the words 'new birth' or 'regeneration'. You will then be able to trace the development of concept through the appropriate Scriptures, and be assured that the whole Church is caught up in the new birth which the Holy Spirit works in the human heart and within the community of God.

This redeems the term 'born again' from misuse – indeed, that little nun could have quoted one of the liturgical collects for Christmas, which puts the term into its proper context:

> Almighty God,
> you have given us your only-begotten Son
> to take our nature upon him,
> and as at this time to be born of a pure virgin:
> grant that we, who have been born again
> and made your children by adoption and grace,
> may daily be renewed by your Holy Spirit;
> through Jesus Christ our Lord. Amen.

So if you have been moved in love by the Holy Spirit, and baptised into the Church of Christ, then the powers of the new birth are at work in you, and you are born again! You may not want to identify with a group

7

or party spirit by using the words, but don't let go of the experience, for it is by grace and love that we are born into the people and family of God.

Reflection

Let us meditate on these words written by the seventeenth-century mystic, Angelus Silesius:

> Though Christ a thousand times
> in Bethlehem be born,
> If he's not born in thee,
> thy soul is all forlorn.

3

Theological Training – Heresy and Devotion

Q *My years in theological college give me great pleasure, but my busyness has caused me to lose my way in terms of intimacy with Christ. I do want to love Christ more, and my mind and heart are open to all kinds of questions. Some of my peer-group Evangelicals have branded me as a heretic, and sometimes I am happy about this, but more often than not it hurts. It seems to me right to hold firmly to Christ, but also to be open in theological enquiry, as in the whole of life. Am I right in my attitude to theological study? (Nic)*

R   Your question is like all our letters, Nic – full of theological, devotional, intellectual and moral questioning, in a mixture of assurance and intellectual stimulation that makes the quest exciting and creative.

Let me respond to *your* question while making such a response applicable to the growing number of ordinands, young priests and pastors who are in touch with me at various levels and with varying Catholic, Evangelical and liberal backgrounds. My relationship with you all is warm and enthusiastic, and this is the context which stimulates great reciprocity in theological exchange and in our mutual life of prayer. Growth and maturity must be linked with intellectual honesty and a deep devotion to Christ. The wonderful thing is that differences of opinion can actually deepen friendships!

There is no need for me to tell you that if you are too busy to pray, then you are simply too busy! Stop some of your activities, organize your life around priorities, and make time and space for contemplative prayer. A great deal of my early theological training was spent in wrangling and scoring theological points against the liberals! And a lot of good it did them – or me!

A warm gospel faith has its Catholic, Evangelical and intellectual dimensions, and you will understand when I affirm with Simone Weil:

> Christ likes us to prefer truth to him because, before being Christ, he is truth. If one turns aside from him to go towards the truth, one will not go far before falling into his arms.[1]

During my own theological training I found myself increasing in evangelical awareness of the Gospel, but I had to throw away much of my fundamentalist baggage because intellectual integrity demanded it. You are finding, as I did, that some will think you too evangelical, while others will think you have turned heretic, and the latter will be afraid that your ecumenism compromises the Gospel. The truth is that this manifests growth in grace and knowledge, and at the same time you will be more sympathetically human.

The period of theological training will pass too soon, so every opportunity should be taken to be intellectually open and adventurous in exploring our faith and its universal application in the world. To be trained in 'the cure of souls' is to learn to be a physician to the whole person.

You will continue to meet with those whose opinions differ from your own – so engage with them in vigorous debate, but always be a person of integrity and reconciliation. This will be no easy task, but it will pay immense dividends both in your training and in later ministry in the Church and the world. I have voluble agnostics and atheists among my dear friends!

Reflection
Let's try to get inside the skin of our critics, understand their arguments, note where they are coming from, respect what truth there is in their opinions, and love them despite all.

4

Infallibility?

Q *How can any doctrine of infallibility be equated with a faith that is meant to be dynamic in its revelation of God? Is the problem really concerned with the way in which the word and authority of God is mediated and communicated in the different denominations of the Christian Church?* (*Luke*)

R Before you entered theological college, Luke, and got into enthusiastic and hot debate with Anglicans, Catholics, charismatics and all shades of theological opinion, you held a warm, simple, trusting faith in Christ which had no party spirit attached to it – and perhaps you sometimes look back with yearning to those problem-free days! But they were not free of problems, were they? It is just that the problems are different now, and though your fuller letters keep me on my toes in engaging with a range of exciting theological possibilities, I know that beneath the lively and sometimes controversial debate, your heart is set on the Christ of Scripture who is loved within the fellowship of the Church.

But to address your question. You know well how precarious is the word 'infallible'. What or who is perfectly free from error in our human state? The pope? The Bible? The Church? An ecumenical council? A contemporary charismatic prophet? I hope you appreciate the privilege of your theological journey. You have lived, debated and worshipped with all types of temperaments and churchmanship, and you have learned to respect men and women of integrity, whether you agree or disagree with them. But you also have a nose for hypocrisy and heresy. You have already discovered that there are theologians, priests and pastors who hold different views of Church, Scripture, sacraments and authority, but

10

who hold fast to the centre which is Christ. They manifest devotion to him and compassion in the world – so we are able to learn many good things from those with whom we disagree. I say that because the word 'infallible' stirs up both warm debate and hot dissent. It is refreshing to read Hans Küng on the subject (for example, books like *The Church*, and *Infallibility*),[1] because he knows the glory and pain of being a dissenting theologian within the Catholic Church, and we may imbibe from him a genuine sympathy for the broad spectrum of opinion.

I feel it is a pity that the word 'infallibility' gained such prominence, for it is authority with which we are concerned. When we read historical theology and rub shoulders with ecumenical groups in dialogue and worship, we increasingly realize that we are human and fallible at every level, and that only God is infallible. The mediators of God's will may bear different levels and modes of authority, but it is salutary to note that those who insist on infallibility become exclusivist in their claims and attitudes.

I like St Vincent of Lerins' famous formula of the basic content of the Christian faith: 'That which has been believed everywhere, always and by all', and lest that sounds like a sort of static definition, he goes on to affirm that

> there should be a great increase and vigorous progress in the individual as well as in the entire Church as the ages and the centuries march on, of understanding, knowledge and wisdom.[2]

Obviously you want me to come clean as to where I stand, for you know my love of the Catholic and Evangelical traditions, and my respect for intellectual integrity. I do not believe in any human infallible authorities, whether of Scripture, pope, council or charismatic prophet, but I do acknowledge certain authority which may be mediated through these from the risen Christ. Supremely I acknowledge the authority of canonical Scripture, though not its infallibility.

You may remember the name of the great Anglican divine, Richard Hooker. He is an example of what has been called 'multiform authority' in his classic synthesis of Scripture, tradition and reason, with the Holy Spirit moving, working, speaking through each.

My love of Scripture makes me affirm that the Bible is the supreme, though not the sole, authority in matters of faith. It is the 'basic authority' with stable objectivity which gives and preserves the Church's identity.

11

But the community of God is not book-static, it is rather Spirit-dynamic, for the community's faith came before the book, and produced the book. The value of St Vincent's formula is that it indicates that Scripture is interpreted with the mind of the whole community, extended through space and time.

I can almost hear you say: 'Well, that sounds very noble, and perhaps it was possible before the Reformation, or rather before the split between the Eastern and Western Churches. But how can it work now?'

Does it sound strange to you that I would turn to the Orthodox Silouan the Athonite in order to respond? In his teaching 'Concerning Tradition and the Scriptures', he defines sacred tradition as the unceasing action of the Holy Spirit in the Church, and that is the source from which the Scriptures flow. Then comes this remarkable paragraph:

> Suppose that for some reason the Church were to be bereft of all her books, of the Old and New Testaments, the works of the holy Fathers, of all the service books – what would happen? Sacred Tradition would restore the Scriptures, not word for word, perhaps – the verbal form might be different – but in essence the new Scriptures would be the expression of that same 'faith which was once delivered unto the saints'. They would be the expression of the one and only Holy Spirit continuously active in the Church, her foundation and her very substance.[3]

Orthodoxy does seem to me to reflect the life and position of the early Church on the matter of authority, and the above comment represents the dynamic and charismatic work of the Holy Spirit within the body of Christ.

It may be easier to have an infallible book, magisterium or Church, but because of honest sharing and fellowship in dedicated scholarship in these ecumenical days we must rejoice in our own insights and bear one another's burdens. My last word in this response is to commend the dictum of the great St Augustine:

> In things essential, Unity;
> In things not essential, Liberty;
> But in all things, Charity.[4]

Reflection

While remaining faithful to the insights of our own communion, let us inform ourselves, sympathetically and creatively, of those of other theologians and communions in ecumenical sharing and integrity.

5

Understanding the Trinity

Q *I have great difficulty in understanding the doctrine of the Trinity. Can you help?* (Mair)

R You are not alone, Mair. The great St Augustine did not find it easy either. But he did find it exhilarating to explore the nature of the great God of mystery in whom there is unity and diversity, and whose Being overflows into a communion of love, drawing us all back into the ocean of infinite wonder.

Perhaps it's the wrong way round to tackle the doctrine! The disciples had a great Jewish inheritance of a faith which taught them the glory of the one God, and the text which was written in a scroll on their doorsteps, proclaimed in Temple and synagogue, and repeated in liturgical and personal prayer, was the Shema:

> Hear, O Israel: The LORD our God is one LORD; and you shall love the LORD your God with all your heart, and with all your soul, and with all your might (Deuteronomy 6.4–5, RSV).

Then the wandering preacher from Galilee, after his baptism in Jordan and the wilderness temptation, found and called the disciples one by one, until they were drawn into the company of the twelve. The life and ministry of Jesus, his healing miracles and the charism of his preaching and authority, caused them to believe that he was the prophesied and awaited Messiah who was to come and deliver Israel.

There was confusion, bewilderment and cowardice among them at Jesus' betrayal and death, and they were scattered in fear. As Jesus had

13

told them, though they were not able to understand, he came to life in a mighty resurrection, and manifested himself to them in the body in which he had been crucified, but which was now transformed, though still bearing the Calvary wounds. Before finally withdrawing from them in the body, he promised the coming of the Holy Spirit for which they were to wait in Jerusalem.

When the Spirit descended in wind and fire, they were filled with gospel joy and dynamic spiritual life which put to flight all their fears, and imparted a boldness and assurance in preaching Jesus as Messiah.

Here, then, is the basis of a new understanding of the being of God, as experienced by Jewish believers caught up in the wonder of the resurrection of Jesus and the pentecostal Spirit. They believed in and experienced God expressing himself in the life, death and rising of Jesus the Messiah, and in the creative power and indwelling of the Holy Spirit – a threefold pattern which was evident at Jesus' baptism in the Jordan when the voice of the Father spoke from heaven and the Spirit descended upon Jesus in the form of a dove. Then Peter, James and John shared their experience on the Mount of Transfiguration, when the uncreated light of the Spirit irradiated the being of Jesus, and the Father's voice spoke from the cloud of the presence.

In Matthew's Gospel we find Jesus, before his ascension, giving his disciples the great commission: 'Go therefore and make disciples of the nations, baptising them in the name of the Father and of the Son and of the Holy Spirit' (28:19).

So from the day of Pentecost the disciples had to somehow make sense of this triadic or threefold experience of God, manifested in the inherited God of Israel, in the amazing man who made claims of divinity (John 10.33; 14.9–10), and in the power, action and communication of the guiding Spirit among and within them (Acts 1.2–8; 2.1–4).

They did not receive a dogma of the Holy Trinity from some ecclesiastical council, which they had to impose upon a bewildered multitude. It was rather that they were seized, converted, transformed, enlightened and filled with an entirely new threefold *experience* of God, expressed in terms of Father, Son and Holy Spirit. Right through the New Testament this threefold pattern is repeated in experience, spirituality and doctrine. The Trinity was not a dogma presented for intellectual acceptance, but an experience to be caught, lived and communicated in joy and power.

14

Reflecting on this powerful pattern a year or so ago, I decided to go through the New Testament in my 'marked' Bible. So beginning in Acts (later going back to the gospels), wherever I found a reference to the Holy Spirit, I looked for a *specific* mention of the Father (God), and the Son (Jesus, the Christ), and wherever there was an evident association (which was usually the case), I drew a red triangle in the margin.

I have always been a firm, trinitarian Christian, but I was surprised to see the repeated triadic references as the number of red triangles began to grow. There were 30 specific triadic references in Acts, quite apart from the places where it speaks of the Spirit speaking, moving, leading and guiding.

Do you see what I am saying? If you begin your search by *experiencing* God in the pages of the New Testament, and in your personal and sacramental experience, you will find that the unity of God is expressed in his threefold glory, love and communion in such a way that you can see why Paul sums it up succinctly in the apostolic benediction: 'The grace of the Lord Jesus Christ, the love of God, and the communion of the Holy Spirit be with all of you' (2 Corinthians 13.13).

If you want to go from there into a study of trinitarian theology, you can examine how the doctrine of the Holy Trinity came to be formulated in dogmatic terms between the canon of Scripture and the Council of Nicaea in AD 325 – but that is a matter for another day! Begin with your experience of God in holy Scripture – and even if you stay there and 'overflow' in love and proclamation, you cannot go far wrong!

Reflection

All the above is true and valid – but it is an immense joy to see the way in which John Macquarrie deals with trinitarian doctrine, experience and reformulation in contemporary terms in *The Principles of Christian Theology*.[1]

6

Offer of Salvation after Death?

Q In my early years as a Christian, I believed that unless a person believed in Jesus before they died, they would not be 'saved'. This is what I was taught and what I understood from the New Testament. I have come to feel that I cannot accept that death is the cut-off point. Is it acceptable for people to seek God outside the Christian tradition, to die doing so, and then to find Jesus waiting for them on the other side? (Keith)

R Over the years, Keith, we have shared not only a journey of spirituality, but of theological understanding. I know your reverence for the authority of the Bible and of the interpretation of the Christian faith within the discipline of the Church of God. We have shared similar concerns at different points of the journey, and I would like to relate your question to the following groups of people who have led me to raise the issue:

- What of those who have never heard the Gospel of Christ?
- What of those who have heard the Church's preaching but have been so put off by its exclusive and judgemental image of God that they have rejected such preaching?
- What of those who have examined the Church's persecutions, crusades and hypocrisy and have turned away in disgust?
- What of those who have been brought up in other cultures and traditions and have become loving and moral Hindus, Buddhists, Muslims, Sikhs, etc?
- What of those who have wanted to believe, longed for faith, greatly sought after God, and yet have never received light, inward peace or assurance of forgiveness?

I have recently been writing about the two criminals who were crucified with Jesus (Luke 23.32–43), recalling that they responded to Jesus in entirely different ways. My thoughts on them address this question directly:

Here is the mystery of human choice and responsibility. Jesus hangs there on the cross both to *open* the gate of Paradise, and to *guard* the way from eternal darkness. Jesus did not reject the thief who reviled him, but included him in the covering love of Calvary, forgave him freely for his insurrection, derision and rejection. But what Jesus would not, could not, do was to compel him to enter Paradise . . .

Both these crucified men are transfixed in a place where there is no movement, with the same opportunity for grace, the same offer of salvation, simply on the grounds of mercy and unbounded love. The 'good thief' surely did not understand how the crucified Jesus could be king, but he recognized that Jesus was regal, lifted upon the throne of the cross and crowned with dying glory, and he made a leap of faith – where else was there to go? He cried: 'Jesus, remember me when you come into your kingdom', and Jesus replied: 'Truly I tell you, today you will be with me in Paradise' (Luke 23.42–3). How impossible but how marvellously true!

These two seem to be insurrectionists, revolutionaries, and the second one deliberately held on to his mind-set, even as death stared him in the face. He got into such a state of mind and heart that his nationalistic liberation ideology, backed up by violent, political revolution, was the only way of salvation he could envisage. That is what 'messiah' meant to him, and if Jesus was impotent to liberate them from their suffering and predicament and take the kingdom by storm, then he could only despise such impotence, and even in his dying moments cling stubbornly to a philosophy which he seemed unable to relinquish.

Is there hope for such as him? Well I do believe that the only thing that keeps a soul out of heaven is the rejection of love. If ideologies, philosophies and mind-sets hold us in their grip, and if the hypocritical Church does not communicate Jesus' reconciling love and mercy in this life, then perhaps beyond the vale of death there is another opportunity, another communication of God in which the two ways are made perfectly clear. The invitation of gracious love may then be set forth so plainly that the sheer contrast between life and death, light and darkness, truth and error, cannot be confused. If *then* love is deliberately rejected, lostness is thereby freely chosen, and it may be said: 'This is the judgement, that the light has come into the world, and people loved darkness rather than light because their deeds were evil' (John 3.19).[1]

I am suggesting here that the love and mercy of God are not confined to this life, and as I believe that infants and mentally impaired people are covered by the redeeming love of Christ, I would extend such covering to all those who have lived according to their light, with their faces towards God and compassion in this world. They are not saved by their own works of merit, but by the grace of God – yet their attitude of response to light makes this possible. As for those who rejected or turned away from an image of God or the Church which appeared tyrannical or hypocritical, I am suggesting that they will receive the offer and opportunity of seeing the light and love of Christ in perfect clarity. And those who, in this life, have yearned for God and for the gift of faith (some of my friends are among them) will be filled with amazement on the other side of death, and embrace Jesus with joy and love.

I am not preaching universalism – for there may be some (including the second crucified criminal) who will persist in rejection after seeing Christ in utmost clarity – indeed, such clarity may strengthen their rejection! If so, they will, in their turning from love, light and life, fall back or lapse into the opposite – alienation, darkness and non-being. That means that they will simply cease to be. This would be the ultimate reality depicted in all the judgement imagery of the Bible.

There is a great deal to be unpacked in such an interpretation and understanding of the gospel. But I would say that none of this is novel – it is represented in the salvation thinking of the Eastern Fathers of the fourth century and earlier. Present theological thinking, right across the mainstream Churches, frequently runs along these lines. Those who are interested in this might like to look at the Anglican doctrinal report, *The Mystery of Salvation*, especially Section 8: 'Ending the story'.[2]

Reflection

Hell is not eternal torment, but it is the final and irrevocable choosing of that which is opposed to God so completely and absolutely that the only end is total non-being . . . Annihilation might be a truer picture of damnation than any of the traditional images of the hell of eternal torment. If God has created us with the freedom to choose, then those who make such a final choice choose against the only

source of life, and they have their reward. Whether there be any who do so choose, only God knows.
(*The Mystery of Salvation*, p. 199)

7

Will Christ Come Again?

Q *How will Christ come again? Can this be interpreted to mean that Christ is born again in each one of us as we become enlightened, or in each celebration of Easter?* (*Pete and Judy*)

R Not only is this an important question, but Pete and Judy have already found that it has a number of levels of interpretation. I believe that Christ will return at the second advent to wind up our history and to bring in the kingdom of God – but let me also share other levels of what his 'coming' could mean.

First, Christ came when Jesus was born in Bethlehem. Orthodox Christian faith has a high view of what is called the incarnation. It teaches that the Logos (John 1.1 – a concept also found in Greek philosophy as well as in Hebrew literature), which shared in the eternal threefold being of God, became a human being in Jesus. That was a unique coming into our humanity in order to reveal to us the love of the Father's heart.

After his life of love, and death on the cross, the risen and transfigured Jesus who was the Christ (Messiah), returned to the dimension of the Godhead. We have to use temporal and spatial language to express this because of the poverty of human language, and the limitations of our minds.

The next great event is the Spirit's descent at Pentecost, and this is another sense in which the coming of Christ is made real in the lives of his disciples, and in the Church. When the Church celebrates Easter, as the question suggests, Christ comes in the reality of his risen life, for he said: 'Where two or three are gathered in my name, I am there among

19

them' (Matthew 18.20). And every new believer in Jesus experiences the Easter coming to his or her own heart.

This is also true in every celebration of the Eucharist, and whenever the Bible story makes Jesus real to the believing heart. He comes to us in every moment of our lives, in joy and sorrow, in sickness, and especially in our last moments when we need his loving presence to carry us through death and into eternity.

In all these ways Christ comes – but when the New Testament talks about the *parousia*, or second advent of Christ, it is affirming that all humankind is moving towards the great cosmic event of Christ's return to wind up the historical dimension, to end the warring among nations, to establish justice and initiate his spiritual kingdom of love and peace. There are hundreds of references to the second coming of Christ in the New Testament, and the great creeds of Christendom have all and always affirmed it.

There is no space here to expound its meaning or to warn against wild interpretations, but there are some things which need to be said. First, we can confidently believe that the long-awaited kingdom of God will be brought in, in its fullness, at the second coming of Christ, and that we should live in humble expectation of it.

Second, we must not get involved in fanciful interpretations of the Bible or 'signs of the times', setting dates, or dressing in white and climbing a sacred mountain, as some have done. Many of the sect-like groups on the fringe of the Church have great wallcharts and calculations usually based on the apocalyptic books of Daniel and Revelation, with their own esoteric interpretation.

The fact of Christ's second coming may be affirmed gladly, but the time and manner of that coming is in the will and knowledge of God, and Jesus warned his disciples against involvement in a maze of interpretation (Matthew 24.36; Acts 1.7). The letters to the Thessalonians are full of the subject, and Paul wrote these in explanation, warning the readers of error. The Corinthian believers were also full of questions about Christ's resurrection, the new spiritual body we shall receive in the kingdom and about the *parousia*, or coming of Christ (1 Corinthians 15).

So let your thinking, reading, praying about Christ's second coming be a stimulus to faith and searching, but beware of sect-like prophetical teachings which make incredible claims for contemporary events and persons as fulfilments of odd corners of the minor prophets!

Reflection

Look up in a dictionary of theology the words 'advent', 'coming', '*parousia*', and you will have guidelines for interpretation, and a further list of beneficial reading.

8

God Feeling Tired?

Q *Why did God need to rest on the seventh day, as we read in Genesis 2.2?* (Jo)

R This is a marvellous question, because it enables me to say that I do not aim primarily to *answer* questions, but to *respond* to them, so that new avenues of thinking, questioning and resolution are opened up. In this case, it is a matter of the way in which we read the Bible.

First, let us think about the seventh day. Well, the days of Genesis began before the sun and moon appeared, so they cannot be literal, 24-hour days measured by the sun. In any case, though the book of Genesis is a book of theological truth, it is not a book of archaeological, geological or historical fact. It would be better for us either to think of these days as creative ages or epochs, or understand that the first eleven chapters of the book of Genesis are a series of poetic and parabolic ways of communicating the manner in which God works and speaks among humankind. After all, we must remember that 'with the Lord one day is like a thousand years, and a thousand years are like one day' (2 Peter 3.8).

Second, we must realize that, when the Bible speaks of the way in which God acts towards us, it has to use human language, for we have no other – but it has to stretch it by analogy, metaphor and parable. It engages in what we call anthropomorphism, which means speaking of God in a human form. This is legitimate and necessary, but we must be aware that we are doing it. For instance, we read that the eye of the Lord is upon the righteous and his ear open to their cry, that his arm is

21

outstretched to save, that his hand is upon the prophet, and even that the Lord smells the savour of sacrifices. Yet we know that God does not have eye or ear, hand or arm – indeed, is not in physical shape at all, for God is spirit (John 4.24). We are reduced to speaking of the Lord in human form or remaining silent.

So if God is not physical, he does not get tired, and if he does not tire, he needs no rest. Even that 'he' is traditional, for God does not have gender. Therefore, in the creation work of Genesis, if a day does not mean a day, and God does not get tired and need rest, what can the text possibly mean?

This is not intended to confuse, nor to point up contradictions or naivities in the biblical text – for the text is full of wisdom. But it does mean that we have to learn how to read the Bible, and that though there are parts of Scripture which should be taken literally, factually, concretely, there are other parts which are poetic, parabolic, mythical, symbolic and apocalyptic (using last-day symbolism). The Bible has a canonical unity, but it is also composed of many books, writers, styles, theologies and dimensions. There is no flat level of inspiration, but a multifaceted reflection of the inspiring Spirit working through different authors in different centuries and cultures, and dealing with a collection of problems thrown up by the brokenness and beauty of our world in the light of the eternal wisdom, mercy and grace of God.

Once you take hold of the golden cord of biblical investigation with an open mind, it can lead you into all kinds of unexpected and wonderful places, but guidance is needed (Acts 8.31). As in all things, there are extremes. I have struggled through works of biblical scholarship which are so turgid and frankly uninteresting that they bore your pants off! But there are exegetes and commentators whose abundant gifts of communication and enthusiasm for the text carry you along. They convey an overview which holds together the comprehensive breadth of God's revelation with a perceptive view of a particular passage which clearly discerns God's activity. They can begin with the there and then, and lead inevitably to the here and now.

Biblical criticism is not something to be afraid of, as long as it is constructive criticism based on an open honesty towards the text. My own theology is moderately conservative in a Catholic/Evangelical tradition, so I am very cautious about certain liberal scholars because of the preconceptions which they sometimes bring to the text. But I find myself in creative agreement or disagreement with open-minded theologians who are willing to allow the text to judge them, while not imprisoning the Spirit within the pages of a holy book. I must qualify this, though, by saying that we all bring certain preconceptions to the text of Scripture and must be aware of this in our attempt to be objectively open and honest.

I have given enough of a response to set interested readers on the trail. My own writings are mostly in the area of spirituality, but you will see that they are informed by a clear theological underpinning which depends on the consensus of orthodox, ecumenical, contemporary thinking. If you want some examples of what I mean, look at John Macquarrie's *Principles of Christian Theology*,[1] or if you want a panoramic view of theological thinking, sell your shirt and buy Alister McGrath's two volumes, *Christian Theology*, and *The Christian Theology Reader*.[2]

Reflection
Are we willing to allow our curious minds to lead us on a real theological quest? It will mean the purchase of some basic theological book, and a willingness to give time and effort to disciplined study. But, led by the enlightening Spirit, it will lead us to a mind's appreciation and a heart's devotion to the revelation of God in Christ.

9

Spirituality – What does it Mean?

Q *Sometimes I think of 'spirituality' as the consequences of my Christian belief in prayer and my manner of life (for example, meditation and simple lifestyle). But as I come across the word in religious writings I get confused as to the broadening interpretation of its meaning. Is it possible to have a definition? (Irene)*

R Spirituality is a vogue word, and it is generally used to embrace attitudes, beliefs and practices which enable people to reach out beyond the material world. This is too wide and vague a description to be a definition, and is unsatisfactory for practical use, but it helps as a beginning.

Some Christians don't like the word at all. When Madame Guyon's mysticism was condemned in the seventeenth century as being too refined, rarefied and not sufficiently earthed, it was pejoratively called 'la nouvelle spiritualité' (new spirituality). But soon the word became a blameless term embracing the life of prayer and discipline with the accompanying hopes of higher levels of mystical experience.

The Christian use of the word usually describes the interior spiritual life of the believer, overflowing into a consequent disciplined lifestyle patterned on the example and teaching of Jesus. But it is increasingly used to describe different kinds of ethos within the Christian tradition – such as Franciscan, Orthodox, Ignation or Benedictine spirituality. I was lately pleasantly surprised to receive a book with the subtitle 'Explorations in Evangelical Spirituality' – surprised because the word has been regarded with some suspicion from that quarter.

But there are other spiritualities. One can talk these days of Buddhist spirituality, or Sufi, Hindu or even Aboriginal spirituality. All these may have genuine spiritual insights from which the Christian may profit. But we must also bear in mind that the term itself is neutral, and may even have an evil connotation. People may give themselves, as individuals or in ideological groups, to the contemplation of evil so that it binds them in a fascination of power resulting in manipulation and oppressive evil in the political or religious sphere. As Gordon Wakefield says: 'Adolf Hitler was a spiritual being, a man, more than most, "possessed"; yet his spirit was surely evil'.[1]

There is also a contemporary problem of spiritual restlessness and hunger, and a quest for cheap, mystical 'highs' induced by drugs or stimulated by charlatan elders, shepherds or gurus. These may lead to an emotional or physical cul-de-sac, and I have often found myself picking up the pieces among disillusioned pilgrims.

My own writings fall within the broad definition of spirituality, though I am averse to pietistic and vague sentimentality, or to the emotionalism which occurs in irregular waves throughout the charismatic movement. A true Christian spirituality must be built upon the saving revelation of God in Christ, embracing a disciplined dedication of the heart and mind in prayer and study. Such a spirituality will spill over into social concern in issues of peace and justice, and a mature response in concrete support and leadership in Christian and secular agencies of charitable aid.

Spirituality is concerned with the interior life of prayer and love, and it is for everyone. If genuine, it will lead to an increase in love of one's true self and of brothers and sisters all around. Let me conclude with words of Thomas Merton concerning the novices and scholastics under his care in Gethsemani monastery – depicting a well-earthed spirituality:

> The best of them, and the ones to whom I feel closest, are also the most solitary . . . All this experience replaces my theories of solitude. I do not need a hermitage, because I have found one where I least expected it. It was when I knew my brothers less well that my thoughts were more involved in them. Now that I know them better I can see something of the depths of solitude which are in every human person, but which most people do not know how to lay open either to themselves or to others or to God.
> (*The Sign of Jonas*, p. 328)[2]

The only change Merton would make in that quotation today would be to include 'sisters' in an all-embracing spirituality.

Reflection
Read Gordon Wakefield's article 'Spirituality',[3] and continue to discover the riches concealed beneath the surface of this word.

10

Should Jesus be Worshipped?

Q *I understand that Christ is integral to the Christian Faith as the manifestation of God's love and as the Saviour of the world. But, surely, in the gospels Jesus points us to the worship of God, not of him. And even after the resurrection and throughout the rest of the New Testament, worship is offered to the Father, through Jesus the mediator. Is the worship of Jesus an end in itself or not?* (Malcolm)

R This is a matter of great theological importance! In both Catholic and Evangelical traditions there is such a high Christology that it seems that supreme worship is accorded to Jesus in order to affirm his divinity, and lest his full deity be compromised. My own experience was that when I began my theological education, I discovered to my amazement that I was an Apollinarian (Apollinarius taught that in Jesus the divine Logos took the place of the human soul). In other words, I had been so concerned with the divine nature in Christ that I was actually denying the fullness of his humanity.

It is significant that the eucharistic prayers of all the liturgical Churches are addressed to God the Father, in the name of Christ the Son, by the power of the Holy Spirit. That is the primary way of praying – though of course prayer may be made to Jesus the Saviour and mediator, and to the Holy Spirit as life-giver.

Jesus himself said that he was the way to the Father, and the gospels reveal him always pointing to the Father in his life, deeds and teaching. Jesus is our Saviour, friend and brother, our teacher, example and guru, our mediator and advocate. But it is to the Father that he channels and directs our highest worship and adoration. I don't want to make grades or degrees of worship, but there is a sense in which the early disciples worshipped Jesus when they experienced his risen glory (Luke 24.52; John 20.28) – though some manuscripts of the Lucan text omit the words 'worshipped him'.

The main thrust of the New Testament teaching is that Christ will gather all those who belong to him at his second coming, will subdue all wickedness and death itself, and will then offer all things to the Father, so that God may be 'all in all' (1 Corinthians 15.24–8).

This involves a wonderful trinitarian understanding of our redemption, for we have been moved upon by the Holy Spirit and drawn to Christ our Saviour. We have received forgiveness of our sins and all the blessings of the gospel through the Son, and we are carried by Christ our Saviour, mediator and advocate, into the presence and mystery of God the Father. In experience, this revolutionizes our life of prayer, for we are caught up into the wonder of Christ's communion with the Father – but that is another dimension!

Reflection

William Bright's eucharistic hymn, 'And now O Father, mindful of the love' (*New English Hymnal*, 273), especially Verse 2, printed below, clearly illustrates what we have said above. Does this influence the way in which we think of our relationship to Christ as Saviour, and to the Holy Spirit's ministry in our life of prayer?

> Look, Father, look on his anointed face,
>   And only look on us as found in him;
> Look not on our misusings of thy grace,
>   Our prayer so languid, and our faith so dim;
> For lo, between our sins and their reward
>   We set the passion of thy Son our Lord.

11

Why All the Sin and Misery?

Q *Why is it that some Christians' faith and preaching is all about the fall, sinfulness, wickedness and retribution? Surely sin and wretchedness are not the first and last things that can be said about human beings?* (Mike)

R How right you are, Mike! Sin and wretchedness are neither the first nor the last things which can be said. The Bible begins with the glory and beauty of a creation in which all things, including humankind, were very good (Genesis 1.31), and ends in the garden of Paradise regained, in which the leaves of the tree of life are for the healing of the nations, and the Lord God is the light of heaven (Revelation 22.1–5).

So when we bring the gospel to men and women who know well enough the wickedness in the world and the darkness in our own hearts, we should begin with the creative love of God, the yearning of the human heart toward light, hope and truth, and the beauty of God in the created order, and in all that continues to reflect his glory in our human experience.

We must go on to speak of the fallenness of humankind, with all the evidence of inhumanity in our society, the wickedness and evil of modern warfare and the pollution of our fragile planet – all these are sins against God. But we must affirm the primacy of joy, life, light and beauty. It is from these things that human beings have fallen, for these things manifest the glory of God, and it is the loss of them that makes people so wicked, desperate, unhappy and frustrated. As I have written elsewhere:

> The primary task is to affirm that joy and love are basic, are of the essence of creation. It is a sad commentary on our world that many people have no other place from which to begin than their own alienation, their own sadness, sickness or despair. This is the condition in which they find themselves. And this is the very place where the Gospel of Christ is able to reach them with its message of forgiveness, love and power. But before we plunge into the darkness of sin and alienation, the basic and primary truth of God's creative love needs to be affirmed. God's love and joy expressed in creation are primary; sin and suffering are invasive and parasitical.
> (*Fulness of Joy*, p. 6)[1]

I am grateful to the Lord for the chronology of my religious experience. It began as a child, not with the cerebral or intellectual acceptance of dogma, but with the intuition of the mystery of God in nature, and the simple human love and affirmation of my parents. When I was a boy I would delight in earth, sea and sky along the coast of the Gower Peninsula. There was an immediacy in the experience of mystery, though I would not have called it God. Yet when I later came to a saving knowledge of Christ, I could look back on all this creative joy, warmth, celebration and intuition of mystical presence in nature and relate it to the love of God – for that is what it was! I would not have denied that I had done wrong things, or that even as a child I had sometimes betrayed my deepest feelings, but the primary truth to me was the aliveness of things, the beauty, the joy – as well as the sadness of all that did not fit into this pattern of love and harmony.

This is the context in which I heard of the greatness of the love of God in Christ – the Christ who became man and lived his holy and loving life among us – healing the sick, showing compassion on the lost and saving sinners. I heard of his suffering on the cross to save humankind, and gladly received him as my Saviour and Lord. But this gospel story – of Jesus entering into our darkness to redeem us from its power – was in the context of my earlier understanding of the love and beauty of God, and of the healing life of Jesus. This is the right way round, and if we get things into that kind of perspective we shall not be continually emphasizing sin, rebellion and retribution, though these are part of the whole saving gospel.

These two aspects have been called 'creation spirituality' and 're-demption spirituality'. Both are necessary for a full gospel, and if one of them is missing then the proclamation is one-sided and unbalanced. This is what this question is about. Our next question concerns the other side, so I shall take it up there. But let me suggest here that for many people, it is more productive to begin not with alienation and sin (and I do not play down those realities), but with their sense of yearning, beauty and longing for interior harmony.

Reflection

Take a walk into a place of natural, artistic, architectural or musical beauty today, and endeavour to link our interior longing for balance and harmony with the evident imbalance and disharmony in the world caused by sin. Does the Christian faith correlate its message with both these aspects in our experience?

12

Creation and Redemption

Q *I have been taught that the creation and human beings have fallen from God, and that only by the death of Christ and God's mercy can people be saved. I am disturbed by New-Age teachings which deny our sinfulness and the need to be redeemed. Am I right to be suspicious of New-Age spirituality?* (Ronald)

R There are many New-Age teachings which are unbalanced, naive and downright heretical. But it is not a single package which has to be accept-ed or rejected totally. Some of the concerns manifest a new awakening of conscience in areas of ecology, animal abuse and the affirmation of the joy of being creatively human.

It is a matter of getting the balance right and becoming more, not less, biblical. Look at the previous chapter, for it develops a balanced biblical spirituality of creation and redemption. Our Western Church background (Protestant and Catholic) has emphasized what is called 'redemption-centred spirituality'. This tradition emphasizes the sinfulness of people in a fallen world, and our need for Christ the Saviour, by his cross and passion, to bring us forgiveness and salvation. Because of this sense of fallenness which we all feel in various ways, there has been a distrust of human achievements and creativity, and especially human loving and sexuality. Guilt is to the forefront and a lack of self-esteem is one of the consequences.

The Eastern (Orthodox) Church strongly affirms the redemption of a fallen world through the cross, but there is a greater emphasis on the resurrection, and sin is viewed not so much in a legal or forensic manner as in the West, but in terms of a human–divine relationship, and as the sickness of an organism needing Christ as physician. The healing power of the Eucharist becomes, in this tradition, the medicine of immortality, and redemption is the divinization of our humanity. We become partakers of the divine nature (2 Peter 1.4). In this tradition, the healing and transfiguring grace of Christ by the Holy Spirit shines throughout creation, redeeming and renewing, and the anticipation towards the coming of Christ in glory involves the renewal of the whole cosmos.

We need to bring together creation and redemption in a biblical manner. I've written of this in *Fulness of Joy*:

> Sadly, in Western theology, we have often set the problems of fallenness and human sin before us in all their stark nakedness and depravity *before* the good news of the Gospel. Of course the Gospel *is* good news to a lost and sick world, but the whole scheme of redemption is far wider and more profound in its context and implications than simply a plan of rescue. We should not begin with the fallenness of creation and the sin of man, but with the goodness and innocence depicted in the paradise story of Genesis.
>
> The goodness of creation as it came from the hand of God is proclaimed in the book of Genesis before the story of the Fall. Man is innocent before he is fallen, and we should affirm the original basic

goodness of the created order *before* we take cognisance of the fallenness and alienation which face us in the world. The way back to that original innocence in which the *imago Dei*, the image of God, is to be restored, is the way of redemption. It is to that fallenness and restoration through Christ that we now turn – from the original paradise, through paradise lost, to paradise regained. And as we take this path we should recognise our own personal and corporate experience in the pilgrimage. As we trace the theological trail, it becomes a path of inward experience. We have glimpses of our own original innocence, a sad awareness of our sinfulness and alienation, leading to the profound experience of joy in redemption.[1]

If we get the balance right, then we should not be afraid of the eccentricities and heresies of much New-Age teaching. We would be able to affirm the image of God in the human heart, with its wistful yearning for wholeness, beauty, truth and innocence, and yet realize that this image has been broken, distorted, cracked and marred (though not completely obliterated) by sin. This would lead us, by the grace of God, to Jesus, the Saviour who is able to forgive us and reconcile us to God in redemption, and then transfigure and recreate us and our world in his image and likeness.

In this way our obsession with guilt and sin would be removed, we would be able to accept and love ourselves as human beings who are loved, and it would enable us to find God in all the beautiful and creative arts, sciences and disciplines of our world which reflect the glory of God. It would also enable us to stand against all that denies and abuses God's glory in the human and animal world and in the natural environment. In a word, it would be a more whole and biblical faith.

Reflection

If we bring creation and redemption together in our understanding of practical spirituality, it will enable us to act in a more loving, wholesome and trusting relationship with people, and to see more of God in all that is beautiful in the world of music, art, poetry, and the creative arts and sciences. What *practical* difference would this make to our attitude to animal abuse and the pollution of our planet? Would we see these as theological matters?

13

Intellect, Emotion and Intuition

Q *I find it strange that I have committed Christian friends whose faith is very cerebral, and yet they are not willing to use their brains in researching biblical scholarship. And others who are charismatic and emotional, and yet they divorce their emotions from their intuition. How can we get 'mind and heart' in good balance and harmony? (Michael)*

R Two illustrations from my experience come to mind, prompted by this question. The first is of a friend whose bookshelves are stacked with volumes by Puritan divines, very heavy and cerebral material. But if you asked him to look at the creation and Eden stories of Genesis as other than literal, or to consider the discrepancies in the resurrection narratives, he would treat such suggestions as heretical.

The second illustration is of the occasion when, as a lad of 17, I went on a coach outing with the local Pentecostal group to one of the Gower beaches. 'Look at that wonderful sunset', I said to one of the older men. 'I don't think you should admire the sun like that' he answered. 'It sounds pagan.' My amazed response was: 'Whose sun is it?'

Here is a dual problem. Some Christians are afraid to use their minds to investigate things theological because it may lead them into conflict and doubt – questioning the very source of revelation. Therefore they shut down on any study which savours of scholarship and criticism. These are sometimes people who are willing to investigate other matters, revealing that they do not lack the ability to think.

This is really a fundamentalist mind-set which will only operate within the covers of the holy book. This is not to be a biblical Christian, but to be bound by the dead letter – and that is what the Bible becomes within such a ghetto mentality (2 Corinthians 3.6).

Such a mind-set can justify, by Bible quotation, such things as apartheid, witch-hunts, inquisition and holy war. Criticism is a word which frightens such Christians, but criticism can be positive as well as negative, and the misuse of literary criticism does not argue for its abolition, but its dedicated use. We cannot believe that every part of the Bible involves a flat level of inspiration or we should be stoning adulterers and executing the sabbath breaker. God has given us enquiring minds, and to discern the human element within the divine revelation, and the growth and purification of that revelation in the Bible, takes an enlightened mind and a devoted heart.

Other Christians, however, are emotional in things religious and are enthusiastic about things charismatic, but they cannot differentiate between emotion and intuition, and they are afraid of any creation spirituality which may indicate that the Holy Spirit is the source of the natural world, and of the creative impulses which give rise to wholesome sexuality, music, art, poetry – indeed all things life-giving and beautiful.

Such Christians fail to differentiate between emotion which is based on sentiment, and the intuitive faculty which has an affective element, but which is informed by a mind enriched by wisdom. This gives rise to knowledge and experience based on intuition rather than on rational intellect. The intuitive dimension is a creative one, and can apprehend the divine presence in the cycle of the seasons, the measure of poetry, the rhythm of music and in all the good and creative disciplines of our human life, including physical sexuality and love which expresses the goodness and wisdom of God. Often in the history of the Church, emotionalism has been rampant, as in the second-century Montanist heresy, with its charismatic prophets who had no recourse to sound, intuitive wisdom. In our own day many good people have found in the Toronto Blessing a real work of the Spirit in freeing them from a cold and buttoned-up cerebral faith, giving them an emotional response which has imparted a new liberty. But the same movement has also given rise to emotional excesses which drive other Christians away and are counterproductive to onlooking non-believers.

We must be willing to open up our minds to the intellectual disciplines of biblical scholarship, believing that God can lead us deeper into truth, and not further from it, by the exercise of our intellectual faculties. Then we must be able to nurture our emotional and intuitive faculties by learning to be open to human relationships and a sharing of our feelings, together with an appreciation of the Holy Spirit as the life-giver in the arts and sciences. For if God is Lord at all, he must be Lord of all.

Reflection

For an appreciation of biblical scholarship, the theological articles in *The New Jerome Biblical Commentary* are recommended;[1] so too is Raymond Brown's book, *An Introduction to the New Testament*;[2] for an enrichment of emotional and intuitive faculties, look at Michael Mayne's book, *This Sunrise of Wonder*;[3] and for a demanding and rewarding theologian any of the writings of Hans Küng.[4] All these books will indicate further reading material.

14

Faith or Works?

Q *Paul's writings clearly state a gospel of grace, but this is much harder to see in the actual words of Christ. His words seem to point to salvation by works, unless we interpret them in the light of Paul's teaching, which is like putting the cart before the horse. Is a gospel of grace actually what Jesus taught? (Nicholas)*

R A marvellous question! Perhaps Martin Luther had this problem when he called the letter of St James an 'epistle of straw'! It is not that we have to interpret the compassionate words and acts of Jesus through the forensic justification language of Paul; nor is it that (putting the horse before the cart) we should follow the compassionate works of Jesus in spite of Paul's juridical teaching of grace through faith alone. Rather we should take off our Western and Reformation spectacles!

What I mean is that in the past we have set the 'salvation by works' Roman theologians against the 'salvation by faith' Reformers, pitting one lot against the other in an either/or situation. This is being rectified in some quarters, for it is increasingly common to find a unifying theological vision among both groups of theologians, appreciating each other's emphases.

If we look at the Eastern Orthodox Churches which had no Reformation on the faith versus works problem, we see that they did not have to take away from the responsibility of humankind in order to add glory to the sovereign God, nor detract from sovereignty to affirm human freedom.

The beauty and majesty of the God of love, from whom all grace and goodness flow, is central in Orthodoxy. Human response in salvation is as much a gift of the Spirit as good works which flow from the same source. This is a biblical theology which reaches back beyond the Reformation and beyond the schism between West and East in the eleventh century. It reflects the theology of the Greek Fathers who themselves drank from the sources of the apostolic teaching.

We do not think that, in order to allow the prodigal son the freedom to return from his dissolute life and retrace his steps to the father, we have to subtract from the loving concern and gift of the father's grace. There is operating here, as in the gospel as a whole, a divine synergy. This word means the working together of the Holy Spirit with the mind and heart of God's erring child. It is not a matter of 'by faith' or 'by work', but of the Holy Spirit who stirs the human heart to yearning and repentance, in order that the sinner may turn freely to the Father, and henceforth walk in the way of loving holiness. It is a matter of faith initiating works, and works following faith – though both flow from the Holy Spirit working through human freedom. St Paul and St James are saying the same thing from different vantage-points, and they both acknowledge the Holy Spirit as the source of grace and goodness.

We must also realize that there is an immense difference of emphasis and evangelistic practice between the revelation of the divine love in the life and teaching of Jesus, and Paul's application of the inherent claims of Christ to the Gentile world with its religious and philosophical climate. We must be cautious about separating Paul from Christ, remembering always that it is Christ alone who is saviour, and from him alone flows the divine compassion to all people everywhere, purely on the basis of human need.

When we enter into the mystical tradition, whether in the context of the Orthodox, Catholic or Reformed Churches, there is unanimous affirmation of the divine love as the source and goal of all our strivings. All holiness follows from the divine love expressed in overflowing grace – and the believer and the Church are alike caught up into that divine mystery. This puts the theological party quarrels among the Churches into the context of eternity, where God is alpha and omega, and humankind is caught up in the schema of redemption, and into participation in the divine life of the Trinity.

Reflection

Resolution in a nutshell: 'Work out your own salvation with fear and trembling; for it is God who is at work in you, enabling you both to will and to work for his good pleasure' (Philippians 2.12–13).

15

God of Hatred, God of Love?

Q *Can we take the Bible at face value as a revelation of God's character when we read of such things as the killing of Saul's innocent descendants to avenge the Gibeonites (2 Samuel 21), the plague on Israel following David's presumption (2 Samuel 24), and the stoning to death of the man gathering firewood on the sabbath (Numbers 15)? How do these awful incidents (and many like them) tie in with the proclamation of God's love and gentleness?* (Brian)

R I know that you have struggled with these and similar passages in your theological pilgrimage, Brian, wanting to affirm the authority of the Bible, and the amazing love of God in Christ. Let me tell you how light came to me with the growing realization that the whole Bible should be viewed from the vantage-point of Christ, who expresses the fullness of God's nature and character.

As a young man of 17, I was faced with conscription to military service, and was convinced in my own mind – as a human being, and as a Christian with a saving experience of Christ – that I could not take up arms and be trained to maim and kill others.

As I prepared to state my case in a public legal tribunal (a scary prospect at that young age), I looked at the Bible's teaching on the nature of God. What kind of God did I believe in, and what was his will in terms of military might and warfare?

The passages you refer to (and many others) seem to portray God as a sanguine deity who encourages holy war and crusades, with the extermination and massacre of whole populations – the hating of enemies 'with a perfect hatred'.

I first of all saw this in stark contrast to the Christ who taught love of enemies and who did not join in or encourage various messianic revolutionaries (in the Maccabean tradition), even though his country was occupied by the heathen Romans. He lived and preached forgiveness, reconciliation and peace, and even in his violent death he prayed for those who crucified him: 'Father, forgive them; for they do not know what they are doing' (Luke 23.34).

As I prayed, studied, took counsel and asked for divine guidance, it became clearer that there was not so much a contradiction of two starkly opposing views of God, but rather the emergence of an evolving understanding of the nature of God according to the people's capacity and insight, until the fullness of God's revelation in Christ.

On this pattern, Moses' reaction to the harsh heathen judgement of avenging evil with 'a *life* for an eye . . . a *life* for a tooth', was that of rough tribal justice – only 'an *eye* for an eye . . . a *tooth* for a tooth'. When Jesus quoted these words, it was in the context of revolutionary teaching on forgiveness and reconciliation, culminating in the words: 'Love your enemies and pray for those who persecute you, so that you may be the children of your Father in heaven' (see Matthew 5.38–48).

So it was that, in the midst of thinking and praying through the whole matter of the nature of God at 17 years of age, I began to see the pattern of 'progressive revelation' with the ultimate interpretation of the character of God in the light of the life, teaching and death of Jesus.

So much of what is written in the Old Testament reflects the rough-and-ready perception of wandering nomads, with both beautiful and terrible views of local and tribal deity. At certain times there were high points of revelation given to some of the major prophets, communicating an understanding of the justice and universalism of God's ways with humankind that has never been surpassed (see, for example, Isaiah 11.6–10).

So I became wary of the word 'infallible', which is part of the mind-set of fundamentalists of all kinds, and was suspicious of doctrines and practices which were based upon proof-texts from such books as Leviticus, Joshua or Obadiah!

Over the years I have treasured the revelation of God in Scripture, and affirmed the authority, though not the infallibility, of the Bible. I am indebted both to the biblical critics and to the mystical tradition which built upon my evangelical experience. This saved me from many an error in taking the Bible at face value, for that would have been superficial and foolish.

In the fellowship and teaching of the wider Church we dig down beneath the surface, evaluate the whole canon of Scripture in the light of the person and teaching of Jesus, and see the progressive nature of God's revelation, guided by the Holy Spirit. God's nature reflects mercy *and* judgement, but his judgement is always in chastisement and with a view to correction. These themes will continue in the following chapters.

Reflection

We must be prayerful and discerning in our study of the nature and character of God in the Bible, always looking into the face of his Son Jesus, to understand the heart of the Father (John 14.8–11).

PART TWO

Questions of Spirituality

16

Lack of Faith, so no Healing?

Q *Some Christian friends have told me that if you are not healed after receiving ministry at a healing service, it is because of a lack of faith, and this has caused some people to feel guilty. Doesn't this create a worse situation than before they sought healing?* (Marjorie)

R Yes it does, Marjorie! What a sad situation to create. I know that there are groups of people who teach that healing is like forgiveness, and that if we fulfil the conditions, then healing must inevitably follow. This is dangerous and heretical teaching, for not only is it unbiblical and contrary to experience, but (as you say) it can add to the suffering of the sick person by piling guilt upon sickness.

Here again, there are two extremes between which we must walk a middle path. One extreme says that although there were miraculous healings and charisma in the early Church, giving it an initial boost, as soon as the apostolic age ended, then God withdrew all such gifts and signs in order that the believer should walk by faith alone.

The other extreme maintains that miracles abound, and that anyone who has sufficient faith can be healed – using words like 'six easy steps to a miracle'!

As in so many cases, both these extremes appeal to the Bible, but in different ways. The first one tends to divide the revelation of God into epochs or 'dispensations', and neatly packs away the age of miracles into the apostolic period, looking with suspicion on any charismatic manifestation, either from the Catholic or the Evangelical traditions.

The second sees angels and devils in every corner, and wants to exorcise the demon out of anyone who suffers from epilepsy or mental illness. Exaggerated claims raise people's expectations and then disappoint them, with the added burden of guilt because of a lack of faith.

The first group forgoes the inheritance of Pentecost, and the joy of seeing God at work in charismatic or sacramental healing of body and mind; their approach makes for a cerebral and rigid religion lacking joy and dynamism. The second group lives in an unreal world, and some turn towards charlatanism, with the problems which have beset the television evangelists of the United States.

The apostle Paul subscribed to neither of these extremes. He himself bore some infirmity which he called a 'thorn in the flesh' (2 Corinthians 12.7). He referred to a physical weakness and mentions some problem with his eyesight (Galatians 4.13–15; 6.11), and he left a co-worker, Trophimus, at Miletus because he was ill (2 Timothy 4.20). He knew that although God does not send sickness, he can bring positive good out of it, and make his power known through human weakness.

This middle way indicates that we should accept that God can, and sometimes does, give positive help and healing of body and mind in answer to prayer and sacramental ministry – but there is no inevitability about it. And certainly, whether or not such healing occurs, it does not reflect the amount or quality of the sufferer's faith. The faith which we exercise should be of the kind which says: 'Grant to your servant, Lord, healing of body and mind, and the alleviation of pain and suffering . . . Nevertheless not my will, but yours, be done.'

In my own life I have received sacramental healing ministry on two occasions, and have taken part in charismatic healing services; as a priest I have anointed the sick and dying in the context of the Eucharist – but I have often been faced with intractable and terminal illness which posits immense questions. I have also witnessed in some suffering people a radiance, patience and joy that seems to have been God's gift to them in the midst of their troubles, and this has not only sustained them, but has communicated itself to those who have ministered to them.

If I were diagnosed with a serious illness I would gratefully accept the ministry of the medical profession, but I would also request anointing and the laying on of hands at the Eucharist, and humbly request healing (James 5.14). If it were granted, I would be gently grateful; and if not, I should seek strength and guidance for the remainder of my life, and ask for a good and gentle death.

There is enough here to give positive guidance in answer to this question, and also to prepare our own thinking for whatever may come our way. Let us share it with friends who may be carrying unnecessary guilt. They may find that the guilt and anxiety which they bear could be causing some of the physical symptoms from which they may then be delivered.

Reflection

Meditate upon this prayer which the priest or pastor may say after confession and as the penitent is anointed.

N., I anoint you with oil in the Name of the Father and of the Son, and of the Holy Spirit. **Amen.**

As you are outwardly anointed with this holy oil, so may our heavenly Father grant you the inward anointing of the Holy Spirit. Of his great mercy, may he forgive you your sins, release you from your suffering, and restore you to wholeness and strength. May he deliver you from all evil, preserve you in all goodness, and bring you to everlasting life; through Jesus Christ our Lord. **Amen.**

17

Nodding Off in Prayer

Q *Before sleeping I feel the need to recollect and centre myself on God as I review the day and pray Compline. However, this often makes me relax so much that I fall asleep before finishing Night Prayer. If, on the other hand, I don't meditate beforehand, Compline is rushed and uncentred, and I haven't really prayed, except by intention. Any thoughts about this?* (David)

R I know you to be a Christian full of dynamism and activity, David, so I wouldn't be surprised if you were ready to fall into bed at the end of the day, and perhaps this is not the time for long meditation in a warm, dimly-lit room in a comfortable chair or on a soft carpet! I know of one fellow who used to say Compline while tucked in his duvet – he had a similar problem to yours!

I have two suggestions. One is to change your meditation time to the morning. Alternatively, if you are too much a night person and if you want to reform your present practice because it is positive, then why not learn to sit either in a cross-legged posture (as in the modified 'perfect' yoga posture), or use a prayer-stool. This will give you a good upright, straight-backed posture which is nevertheless relaxed, and which does not lend itself to soporific meditation, but to alertness.

Let me describe my evening Compline. I leave my 'living hut' and go to my chapel hut, and this going out sometimes involves on-the-spot exercise and deep breathing for a few minutes, which is good meditation preparation. In my chapel hut I have votive lights burning before the icons, the floor is carpeted and I sit on my prayer stool. Sometimes I observe a time of silence and then sing the Compline hymn, 'Servant of God remember' (*New English Hymnal*, 80). Then I say or sing Compline from our SSF office book,[1] followed by a time of silence which varies each night.

My second suggestion may appeal to you for occasional use. I have recorded myself saying and singing Compline, followed by the traditional '*Salve Regina*', and after my opening meditation and hymn, I simply listen to Compline, responding to any particular part of the office, often accompanying it.

I don't know if this sounds a bit eccentric, but it works well for me, and it leads me into a particularly joyful pool of silence. I often find that actually listening (especially to Psalm 91) brings out shades and dimensions of meaning which are sometimes quite overpowering. All this is within the laying to rest of my own body and soul, and commending to God the grieving, suffering, tortured, imprisoned and dying people throughout the world. At the conclusion of the second recorded form, I include a selection of traditional collects which draw the whole world into the embrace of God's love. Because they are recorded, I don't have to put the lights on and go leafing through books, but simply sit on my prayer stool with full attention, allowing the prayers to wash over me and to be prayed in and through me. In the Reflection below I have quoted one of them which last night I found very moving as I listened to it repeated slowly in the dimly-lit chapel of my hermitage.

Reflection

Take care, dear Lord, of those who work, or watch or weep this night,
   and give your angels charge over those who sleep.
Tend the sick, Lord Christ; give rest to the weary, bless the dying,
   soothe the suffering, pity the afflicted, shield the joyous;
and all for your love's sake. Amen.

18

Finding a Spiritual Guide or Director

Q *Is it essential to have a spiritual guide or director other than the Holy Spirit as I seek to live closer to God? If so, how can I be introduced to one? (Jean)*

R I like the way in which you have framed your question, Jean, for you realize that only the Holy Spirit can be our supreme guide in spiritual direction, and that the Spirit's ministry is the essence of what it is all about. But right from the beginning, within the Body of Christ (that is, the Church), there were mutual ministries between believers, not simply from ordained or elected leaders but in simple soul friendship.

There are certainly dangers in this, for there have been autocratic 'directors' who have demanded obedience from penitents in the Catholic tradition, and there have been 'covering shepherds' in the Evangelical and house-church movements who have even dictated details of believers' lives at an intimate and personal level. These are abuses and should be resisted. No believer should be childish and gullible, and God never asks us to resign our thinking faculties to another. That said, there is something very precious in sharing spiritual discernment, whether it be called direction or guidance, and 'soul friend' is a description which indicates related warmth and depth in bonds of fellowship. Some time ago I made a brainstorming list of what is needed in such ministry, and I include it here. You are my soul friend if:

- as a mother or father you love and care for me in my spiritual childhood;
- as a brother or sister you open yourself to me as I to you in complete trust, with no holds barred, in mutual help, laughter and tears;
- as a spiritual physician you diagnose and prescribe for my soul's good;
- as a fellow-pilgrim you take my hand, negotiating the obstacles, perplexities and ecstasies of our shared journey;
- as a wounded healer you listen, with understanding and counsel of the prayer-tradition, to my thinking mind and my yearning heart;
- as a confessor and believer-priest you mediate God's loving forgiveness and constant direction on the way of holiness and humanity.

I have acted as soul friend to others and have received such ministry myself. Under God, I have found it necessary and encouraging. Over the last 20 years so many people have sought such guidance that there has been a dearth of people who have been trained. Although this ministry is a gift of the Spirit, yet there is also need for a disciplined training and recognition to avoid the abuses referred to above. The National Retreat Association (NRA) and its magazine *Vision* has come to the rescue (see 'Useful Addresses' at the back of this book), and it is so good that there is now a training scheme which not only can put you in touch with a reliable and appropriate soul friend for yourself, but which can offer training so that you can take up this ministry if that is where the Lord is leading you. The courses vary in length and depth, from a day (or evenings) per month to a three-year course. Each year the NRA runs a day consultation for those leading such training courses, and produces a leaflet, *Choosing a Spiritual Guide*.

Such a ministry used to be confined to priests, pastors or Religious, but they do not always have the *particular* gifts for spiritual direction, whereas some lay people are greatly blessed in this area. One word of caution (though you are safeguarded within NRA): make sure that the man or woman to whom you go is not self-appointed, with a hidden immaturity, for this work sometimes draws people who desire to manipulate or have power over others because of their own inadequacies.

Reflection

Think on these words from Paul to Timothy: 'You then, my child, be strong in the grace that is in Christ Jesus; and what you have heard from me through many witnesses entrust to faithful people who will be able to teach others as well' (2 Timothy 2.1–2).

19

Scared of a Monastery?

Q *I should like to come and spend a few days at a monastery, or even go on a retreat – but I'm scared, for I wouldn't know what to do, and whether I could stick it out – especially the silence and the religious expectations.* (Terry)

R Many people feel considerable anxiety and apprehension if they've not been on retreat before. Let me assure you, Terry – and others – that you will love it!

A retreat will be helpful to devout Christians who have a warm and responsive love for our Lord – especially if you enjoy reading, walking, fellowship and worship, and spending time in quietness with the Lord. You'll find all those things here in this monastery, perhaps in a different measure and proportion to what you are used to, and in a different style, but you'll soon get into the swim of it – and return again.

But let me make one or two recommendations. I have written a book, *Deeper into God*,[1] which deals with retreats, and you could look at *The Vision*, the annual magazine of the National Retreat Association (NRA) (address at the end of this book). The NRA has Anglican, Baptist, Catholic, Methodist, URC and Quaker member groups, and the magazine lists some 200 retreat-houses and addresses throughout Britain in monasteries, convents and retreat centres. There are retreats for beginners and various age-groups, with workshops and themes from music to calligraphy, painting to iconography, there are healing, fasting and silent retreats – but all geared to prayer and development of the spiritual life.

I have the present issue of the magazine before me, and it is a mine of information, spiritual counsel, and descriptions of Ignatian, Myers-Briggs and Enneagram retreats. Andrew Nash, the editor, writes:

> It was in 1989 that I made my first individually guided retreat. I approached it with excitement and apprehension, taking books and art materials in case of boredom and reminding myself that the car would make escape possible. Like so many, though, I took to it almost immediately, relaxing, as it seemed, into my natural milieu. A life-changing experience, in large measure because of the gentleness, sensitivity and humour of my guide. The retreat was a thing of wonder: and not the least wonderful aspect was that this experience had been available for years without my being the least aware of it. Since then, I have gradually become more involved with retreats, both as a retreatant and as a retreat-giver.[2]

From there, you should go on to consider a soul friend or spiritual guide (see Chapter 18). To have someone to whom you can go in confidence and trust, opening your heart, sharing joys and tears, checking your guidance and taking stock of your progress (or otherwise) at regular intervals.

In the Celtic tradition, the soul friend burns you! We need sometimes to be burned with honest and clear discernment for our own good – I wonder if that is what people are really scared about in going on retreat? I have found such salutary advice both a stimulus and a restraint on my actions.

Well, there you are. There are plenty of opportunities to begin with an open retreat, with plenty of space and freedom for you to get used to it. Then next time you might like an individually guided retreat, or might wish to join a community retreat on a healing or another theme, with addresses, silence and ministry.

Rather than read more of my glowing descriptions, why not get hold of the NRA magazine, and it will whet your appetite, allay your fears, and make you keen to begin.

Reflection

The retreat movement is being greatly used by God to change and renew people's lives. Why not get hold of the NRA magazine *The Vision*, and use it not only to inform yourself of their ecumenical work, but as a basis of intercession for the movement? You may well find yourself being drawn into such ministry yourself in a renewal and dedication that will dispel all apprehension.

20

Grace and Contemplation

Q *Many of the masters of contemplative prayer were from the medieval pre-Reformation era. In what ways does the theology of grace emphasized by Reformation Churches affect one's view of their teaching and the contemplative way?* (Bob)

R One of the reasons I like this question is that it points out the problems which many Reformed Christians have about contemplative prayer and mystical theology. They get the feeling (and teaching) that somehow all mystics and contemplatives are professing to find a way to God which avoids or evades the cross, and that they are endeavouring to ascend to God by their own merit or good works.

This can become a problem if you look at the early and pre-Reformation Church through the spectacles of Reformation doctrines. Unfortunately, the Western Church did get itself into extreme positions in many areas, and this matter of grace and works was one of them. The Church was certainly in need of reformation, but one of the sad things was that the Reformers were pushed far further than they should have been, and in the event produced a proliferation of local and national Churches, groups and sects, all warring with each other and losing that gift of unity which the apostle called upon us to guard and cherish (Ephesians 4.1–6).

Michael Saward, canon of St Paul's Cathedral, speaking from an Evangelical vantage-point, comments on the appalling consequences of the schismatic tendencies of the Reformers, addressing it to the Evangelical world:

49

World Christianity today has approaching 25,000 Christian denominations and when Christians use the creed and say that they believe in 'One, holy, catholic, and apostolic church', they are either forced in pretending those four adjectives are totally imprecise or that somehow something terrible has happened to the dominical prayer that 'they may all be one'. The fact which most evangelicals simply won't face up to, or even don't know, is that this vast denominational mushrooming has largely come from them. For all practical purposes it is the churches of the Reformation in general, and their descendants in the United States in particular, who have created this enormous self-generating hotch-potch, this supermarket of consumerist independency in which anyone can start up his own show at the drop of a hat. In consumerist, independency terms, it doesn't cause a qualm. The more the merrier, all competing 'in loving fellowship', to cut each other's throats right across the world.
(*The Post-Evangelical Debate*, p. 86)[1]

The Reformers were so concerned to affirm that we are saved by the mercy and grace of God and not by our own works, merits, money or ritualistic religion that they appeared, in crying 'faith alone', to denigrate good works in their scheme of salvation. The Catholic theologians were so concerned about the necessity of righteousness, works of mercy and the grace of the sacraments that they appeared to be saying that these were works of merit which gained us access into the presence and salvation of God.

One can see why the Reformers cried out with Paul, 'Works without faith is dead' – and why the Catholic theologians cried out with James, 'Faith without works is dead'. They were both right. There is no need to take away from the sovereignty of God what one gives to the freedom of humankind. Faith in the mercy and love of God alone justifies the sinner before God, but that very faith is engendered by the Holy Spirit who also promotes good works in the believer – and without such works, faith is shown to be invalid.

Getting back to the original question: the great contemplatives of the pre-Reformation Church taught that the love, mercy and grace of God were the source and fountainhead, and that the life of prayer and contemplation was of grace from first to last. One had to co-operate with that grace, of course – but the contemplative was led along the path by the Holy Spirit. This co-operation was the synergy in which the Spirit and the human will mingled in the life of prayer, which is clearly expressed by St Paul:

> The Spirit helps us in our weakness; for we do not know how to pray as we ought, but that very Spirit intercedes for us with sighs too deep for words. And God who searches the heart, knows what is the mind of the Spirit, because the Spirit intercedes for the saints according to the will of God (Romans 8.26–7).

This synergy is most clearly affirmed by the Greek Fathers of the Eastern Church, and I think a most profitable book for those interested in this question is one which I have been exploring with some of our novices: it is Olivier Clément's *The Roots of Christian Mysticism*.[2] Clément links a whole series of Eastern theologians' quotations with comments of his own, providing a wonderful commentary on the mystical theology of the Eastern Church, saturated with Scripture.

The great joy of sharing the Eastern tradition of mystical theology and prayer with Evangelical or Reformed Christians is that it speaks to us from pre-Reformation days – indeed, from the days of the undivided Church prior to the eleventh century. These mystics have a profound love of Scripture and a sense of the grace, wonder and beauty of God. Here we are freed from the Reformation controversies which were stimulated by the corrupt behaviour and theology of the Western medieval Church and the extreme positions taken by theologians of both sides.

It is refreshing, therefore, to read and experience the contemplative theology of the East (as it is of the Celtic tradition), for contemporary Christians are thereby freed from narrow interpretations and can become more ecumenical in the widest and deepest sense.

Reflection

The Greek Fathers do not use the legal, juridical language of the West in their understanding of salvation and prayer. Their language has to do with relationships, with the healing power of the sacrament for the sickness of the human soul, where the sacrament becomes the medicine of immortality. Clément's book will open up the contemplative path without reference to Reformation controversies, for in the arena of mystical theology they do not arise.

21
Contemplative Prayer Today

Q *For guidance and teaching about the deeper reaches of prayer, in particular mystical prayer, writers typically go back to the early Christian centuries or the Middle Ages. What contribution have Christians of more recent times made to a better understanding of these forms of prayer?* (*Bob*)

R Having made a sort of theological response to the question in Chapter 20, let me now be a bit more practical, but with reading recommendations. Over the last 20 years or so, there has been a tremendous interest in all kinds of contemplative traditions, and the Church is at last waking up to its previous dismal provision of teaching and material on the contemplative way. That is why many Christians who were formerly suspicious of pre-Reformation spirituality are now sharing in the rich contemplative fare that is to be found across the denominational board.

When I was university chaplain in the early 1970s, many young people were voting with their feet and joining Sufi groups, Hindu meditation centres and Buddhist retreats. Among the genuine representatives of these groups there was often much to be learned and shared. But there were also charlatan teachers, and 'footloose and fancy free' types who combined the use of drugs and easy sexual availability with esoteric forms of Eastern meditation. We had one such group who sponged upon the Christian community in Edinburgh and caused havoc on the Isle of Cumbrae.

It must be said that the *good* Sufi, Hindu and Buddhist teachers advocated moral (sometimes celibate) lives, and freedom from drugs and tobacco. At one and the same period I found myself picking up the pieces of young people who had become disillusioned on the hippie and Kathmandu trail, and learning about the genuine Eastern faiths, mainly through my introduction to the life and writings of Thomas Merton. In the university chaplaincy we enjoyed great variety, with teaching on Christian theology, Amnesty International's political concerns, and a

Jesus Prayer group, as well as giving hospitality to a small and sincere Hindu meditation group.

Since that time I have been involved with the writing, teaching and sharing in a broadly based Christian spirituality with an increasing contemplative dimension, and reciprocal friendships with those of other faiths. It has been exciting, creative and difficult!

The Churches have taken a long time to realize their failure to teach contemplative prayer; to learn, then share, then teach, then practise the fruits of contemplation. It is still very patchy, and many Churches still resist such teaching in the mistaken view that, apart from prayers of petition, intercession and praise, other more contemplative and mystical teaching is dangerous at best, and may be heretical and against the simplicity of gospel grace.

As traditional Evangelical and Catholic Christians have been exposed to the writings and practices of contemporary Christian contemplative writers and teachers, much of their apprehension has vanished. With increasing freedom they have realized that it is not enough to experience an evangelical encounter with the saving Christ, and to enter into the corporate and sacramental life of the Church. There is a journey to be made, together and individually, in the path of mystical prayer, and growth in grace is being seen increasingly as a deeper experience of God as well as a more informed theological mind.

Let me mention a few of the communicators of contemplative prayer. First, there are the many books by Thomas Merton, all of which reveal the heart of a man of prayer, and the mind of a social critic involved in relating the great theological tradition of the Church to the meditative practices and social concerns of a universal and contemporary Christian. Although he died in 1968, the Church has still not caught up with him, and though some of his writings are obviously dated, many of them, and especially his voluminous correspondence, have a relevance which continues to amaze those who discover him.

We continue to be blessed with novices in the Society of St Francis, and during their time here at Glasshampton, they come down to my hermitage together for a monthly Eucharist, and on an individual basis for teaching, sharing and reading together in the life of prayer. At present I am exploring with Brother Martin, the Jesuit William Johnston's *Mystical Theology*.[1] Johnston has been a rich source of writing on spirituality over these last two decades, in constant dialogue with Asian and Christian contemplative traditions. This is his most recent (and best) book.

Brother Christopher has completed a degree in psychology, so we are beginning with Christopher Bryant's *Depth Psychology and Religious Belief*,[2] and then moving on to his other interpretations of Carl Jung in the area of the interior life.

I am introducing Brother Oswin to the Orthodox tradition with Kallistos Ware's *The Orthodox Way*.[3] This will enable us to examine the basic Christian doctrines through the eyes of a mystical theologian who knows East and West.

Put these books on your list, as well as some from the Celtic tradition – for example, Michael Mitton, who comes to Glasshampton regularly, has written an excellent introduction to the Celtic saints and their theology in *Restoring the Woven Cord*.[4] And you must not miss the beautiful devotional books on Celtic spirituality by David Adam, especially a life of St Patrick, entitled *The Cry of the Deer*.[5]

Richard Foster, a Quaker writer, draws on a wide knowledge and experience of spiritual devotion in his writings, and the spirituality series of Grove Books offers 60 titles indicating the best of Evangelical thinking on the contemplative theme. Anthony de Mello's *Sadhana*[6] is a basic workbook full of simple, practical spiritual exercises for body, mind and spirit – this book is found wherever the life of prayer is being taught.

I must mention the series of books by the Benedictine John Main OSB who founded the World Community of Christian Meditation. I am just writing a positive review of his daily readings, *Silence and Stillness in Every Season*.[7] John Main's name is an important one in direct response to this question, for Bede Griffiths said that Main was among the most important teachers of prayer in the Western Church today. He died in 1982, but many thousands of people over the world are linked in daily meditation taught in the John Main groups. (The community's address is at the end of this book.)

All this is but the tip of an iceberg, for there are modern presentations of Franciscan, Carmelite, Ignatian and Benedictine spirituality, and the fact you are reading this book is an indication that you are already beginning to answer this question!

Reflection

Think and act! Why not write to the John Main Christian Meditation Centre for their literature. This would be the basis for further reflection and would enable you to discover your nearest meditation group. Perhaps this would be the first step into a new chapter of your life of prayer.

22

Many Routes to God?

Q *Is there one God who can be approached by routes other than Christianity – such as Buddhism and Judaism? How can we judge which are acceptable and which are unacceptable religions without being coloured by our own prejudices? (Judith)*

R We cannot be completely objective, especially if we have been brought up in a warm and joyful Christian tradition, or have later entered into a saving knowledge of Christ which illuminates and strengthens all that is true and loving in our own lives. But we can be delivered from unfair prejudice, and we can learn from friends and scholars of other religions and read their devotional writings.

Concerning the validity and value of other faiths, I have responded in some of the related chapters in this section, but let me give you here a personal response. I was brought up to suspect other faiths, and with such a strong affirmation of Jesus as the only and exclusive way to the Father, the strong implication was not only that there was little if any good in other religions, but that they were erroneous, dangerous, and could result in heathen blindness and damnation.

I have moved a long way since those days, for there are godly and saintly people in other faiths, and I appreciate a great deal of their writings and teachings. But I do not therefore compromise the uniqueness of Christ. He is not another god among others in a syncretistic pantheon.

He is the Saviour of the world and the one who reconciled the world to God by his death and resurrection. Therefore, I believe his redeeming work to be a universal one, not only applicable to Christians.

I believe that any human being, in any of the world's great faiths, who lives in sincere compassion and mercy, is not only enlightened in thought and life by the best of their own religion, but by that very devout path is caught up in the work of the universal Holy Spirit who works wherever there is a seeking human heart.

The enlightening Logos dwells in everyone (John 1.9), and draws people to the Father. All the godly people of the Old Testament, though they lived before Jesus came, were nevertheless ministered to by the pre-incarnate Logos (1 Corinthians 10.4), and included in Christ's redeeming work. And I believe this is true also for all those of other faiths whose back is towards darkness and whose faces are towards love, light and God.

I know that this goes too far for some Christians and not far enough for others, but it does maintain the centrality of Christ and his uniqueness as the world's Saviour, while encouraging and allowing an openness to all those sincere devotees of other faiths.

I am not saying that good Hindus or Sikhs, for instance, are among God's people in spite of their faith, but because of it – for there is a great deal of light and love and truth which shines in their writings, teachings and spirituality. I can take up the writings of Ramakrishna, the stories of the Sufi mystics, or the Eightfold Path of the Buddha, and hear the Holy Spirit speaking words of love and life.

On my bookshelf at this moment I can see books commenting on the Christian faith by the Dalai Lama, the Buddhist monk Thich Nhat Hanh, and the Zen teacher Robert Aitken Roshi.

I came to all this gradually, and it has enabled me to appreciate the revelation of God in Christ at a more profound level. Of course I am aware that there is error, heathen practice, and downright sin in certain expressions of some world faiths – but this is true of Christianity also. After all, it would not be just to compare and contrast the worst of the world faiths with the best of Christianity – or the other way round!

The person who has inspired and informed me most in this huge area is the Cistercian monk Thomas Merton. I would commend his writings to anyone interested in this question. My own appreciation of him is expressed in my book *Soul Friend*,[1] and you will find his many books and volumes of correspondence in almost any Christian bookshop or public library.

Yes, there is only one God, and Christ is the supreme revelation and way to the Father – but the light of Christ shines universally. I find Christ historically and openly in the Christian faith, but I also find the hidden Christ in all that is good, true and wise in the great faiths of the world.

Reflection

Why not take up Thomas Merton's book *The Way of Chuang Tzu*,[2] and discover the delightful wisdom of the Taoist monks and teachers who lived three centuries before Jesus, then offer thanks for its beauty in the light of Christ?

23

Learning from World Faiths

Q *Can we learn from other world faiths?* (Ieuan)

R A direct and succinct question! One of my priest-friends is Roger Hooker, based in Birmingham without charge of a parish and therefore free to develop sharing and reciprocal fellowship with Jews, Muslims, Hindus and Sikhs. When I was Guardian here at Glasshampton monastery he wrote me a warm letter about his retreats, with a sting in its tail:

> Could one think of Buddhist monks visiting Glasshampton, and the friars of Glasshampton visiting the Buddhists? To say more would be an impertinence, but to say less would be a betrayal, so I will shut up!

That was the beginning of visits to the Jewish synagogue, the Muslim mosque, the Buddhist centre and the Hindu and Sikh temples. On a joyous visit to a Sikh temple (which resulted in reciprocal visits to

Glasshampton), we were received courteously, even with gratitude, shared some exotic food and sat in silence and meditation together.

It was nothing new for *us* to remove our sandals at the door, to sit in meditative posture and to share silent meditation, but it was new for *them* to find Christians acting so naturally, showing reverence and courtesy for their religion.

It began a relationship in which, when the Sikhs visited us at Glasshampton, we all sat around the altar, with some visiting Pentecostals who 'happened' to be with us that day! I answered Sikh questions on God, Christ, salvation, meditation and prayer. I spoke gently of the Sikh guru Nanak, and told them of our understanding of Jesus as Saviour, mediator and (in their terms) guru. They took up Franciscan themes in which they felt an affinity, and the Pentecostal pastor's wife said to me afterwards that she felt that the Holy Spirit was with them.

The tables were turned on us on one visit to the Hindu temple in Birmingham when, after a gentle and receptive priest showed us around and we spent some time in quiet meditation, a Hindu woman of some rank turned up. She had recently returned from lecturing on Hinduism in the United States, and we were subject to our first taste of Hindu evangelism. The poor resident priest squirmed with embarrassment, and we smilingly listened and added a few quiet comments at the end. But I did not take up her offer to come and 'lecture us' at Glasshampton!

That incident made us painfully aware of the continual Christian insensitivity which gracious Hindus and others are subjected to by arrogant evangelism by Christians.

But does such sharing and reciprocation accomplish anything? Well, certainly in me it opened up a new attitude in reading and learning about the great world faiths, and led to personal relationships and friendships with those of other traditions. It became impossible, with some of them, to deny that they were moved and influenced by the same Holy Spirit. It seemed to me then, and it has been confirmed since, that there is a kind of remnant in all the great world faiths which consists of spiritual people. These people are not corrupted by the dark areas of their religion (Christianity included), but rather they respond to the love, light and truth which their religion communicates at best, and which draws all such people together in our world in which the real enemies are violence, exclusivism, materialism and genocide.

By such dialogue I do not compromise the uniqueness of Christ as the saviour of the world. Indeed, those I have spoken with do not want a watered-down version of orthodox Christianity, and I do not expect to come to some common agreement on dogmatic or doctrinal definitions – for we are formed in very different languages and thought-forms.

But there is a mutual interchange in which we listen and speak, and then share in silence and meditation together, so that the universal Spirit can bring about a sense of the holy, and a peaceful participation in that which we share. I do believe that the light of Christ, the Logos, shines in all that is true and good in the best of world faiths, and am encouraged when I find such a profound change of attitude in the Vatican II *Declaration on Non-Christian Religions*:

> The Catholic Church rejects nothing which is true and holy in these religions. She looks with sincere respect upon those ways of conduct and life, those rules and teachings which though differing in many particulars from what she holds and sets forth, nevertheless often reflects a ray of that Truth which enlightens all.[1]

I smiled with recognition when I came across Thomas Merton's comments on what had become my experience:

> It is illuminating to the point of astonishment to talk to a Zen Buddhist from Japan and to find that you have much more in common with him than with those of your own compatriots who are little concerned with religion, or interested only in its external practice. (*Mystics and Zen Masters*, p. 209)[2]

The Christian Scriptures contain the revelation of God in Christ, and the Church has received the gospel to proclaim to the whole world. But we must not limit God's love and action exclusively to these holy words or to the Church's perception of the infinite nature of God's love. God does not need to consult us when he desires to communicate himself directly to those whose backs are towards darkness and whose faces are towards light and truth, and therefore towards him.

I shall continue to believe that the eternal Logos who was with the Father and the Spirit before the world began, became incarnate in the historical Jesus. I shall continue to proclaim that this Jesus is the saviour of the world. But I will also rejoice to find the light of the hidden Christ and the wisdom of the universal Spirit in all that is good and true in the world faiths.

And as I believe that the godly people of the Jewish revelation are saved through the work of the cosmic Christ, accomplished in his death and resurrection, so I believe that all godly people of any religion, who seek God sincerely, are also drawn into this redeeming love of Christ, by the same Holy Spirit.

This is a long answer to a brief question, but it is only the beginning. For I believe that during our new millennium we shall experience a new and dynamic sharing and dialogue with all those whose feet are set on this pilgrim quest which is as broad as our humanity.

Reflection

We should encourage friendships with those of other faiths – not with a view to converting them from their own faith in which they are as sincere as we are, but so that we can move towards a mutual sharing and dialogue in which we shall all be enriched.

24

Through Buddhist Eyes

Q *The Buddha said that there are only four 'emotions' he would allow himself – the sublime abodes of tranquillity, loving-kindness, compassion and equanimity. We all have to work with the conversion or transformation of emotions. In what way does your practice enable you to work with everyday emotions towards that letting go of self which allows the working of the indwelling Spirit? It often seems as though Christianity nowadays has gone from the historical extreme of suppressing emotion to that of allowing it free reign. This is a practical question as to the method. (Adrian)*

R I have to recover from the question first, Adrian! I think we start from different places, for the four emotions you list are certainly sublime, and I'm not at all sure that the Christian would see him- or herself moving towards such an expression of spirituality. For the Christian, the pattern is the life, death and resurrection of Jesus, and the whole range of human emotions would still be applicable, though sanctified (including anger). But perhaps I have misunderstood you here.

Let me address the second part of your question. Yes, there has been a swing from the suppression or repression of the emotional life towards 'letting it all hang out'. This can easily be exaggerated, though, and despite the swing of the pendulum, a firm moral and ethical foundation has continued to persist. This is based upon the discipleship of Christ, an expression of the divine love and compassion, and is manifested in a disciplined intellectual and moral life.

And yes, involved in that is a twofold movement of letting go of the egotistic and pleasure-loving desires of the flesh and crass materialism, and a certain passivity in prayer that allows the Holy Spirit's indwelling to be the basis of the spiritual life. Christ is the vine and we are the branches. If we simply 'abide' in the vine, the sap of the Holy Spirit will flow through the branches, and fruit-bearing at various levels will be the result (John 15.1–11). If we live in the Spirit we shall not fulfil the lusts of the flesh.

How is this brought about? Well, the life of prayer and meditation is the primary way in which the believer is sanctified. This is lived out in both corporate and personal dimensions. The corporate dimension is the gathering around the word of Scripture and the altar of the Eucharist, with the subsequent fellowship and sharing. In this way the Christian meets with God in Christ, and the spiritual life thus engendered spills over into works of compassion and service in the world.

The personal dimension is the disciplined life of meditation based on Scripture and the teaching and experience of the Christian mystical tradition. This has been neglected in the Church, but there has been a great resurgence of mystical prayer over the last two decades or so. A debt is also acknowledged to the Buddhist and Hindu contemplative traditions in sharing and dialogue – this is an ongoing and reciprocal experience of joy between us.

If I take the question personally I would say that, apart from the corporate dimension which I've mentioned, the personal dimension for me has been to acquire a technique of contemplative practice which involves sitting, posture, relaxation, breathing and stillness. This is my context for meditation upon scripture, also for saying the Jesus Prayer (similar to a Buddhist's mantra method), and being carried into image-less contemplative silence.

There is a specific mystical path in the Christian tradition which involves the three stages of purgation, illumination, and union – and these have their counterparts in the Buddhist tradition.

Such contemplative practice (I hope!) results in a greater awareness of what it means to be simply human in a world in which there is an interrelated web of being and compassion. The life of the cosmic Christ is thus manifested in daily life by the power of the indwelling Spirit, and this is lived out between persons and societies in a dark and needy world.

Much of this needs to be further explained and perhaps qualified, but it is some kind of a response to a question which comes from a different tradition, with its own language and culture, but manifesting a spirituality in which I recognize the same Holy Spirit of compassion and peace.

Reflection

We must give more thought and attention to the work of the universal Holy Spirit in all contemplative traditions in which compassion is the hallmark of spirituality.

25

Buddhist–Christian Friendship

Q *Contemplation leads us inevitably into 'knowing', at a deep level, our interconnection with all that is. The place of animal life has never been high in Christianity. How have you managed this dilemma, and how is this knowledge played out in your own life? (Avril)*

R You live and speak from the Buddhist tradition, Avril, and that is one of the reasons why you are so good for me!

You tell me that theology, doctrine and intellectual enquiry has not been useful to you in the spiritual life, except perhaps as a necessary step in letting go of the 'thinking mind'. I like what you say in your covering letter to your question:

> Before one engages in the asking of questions and in leading others into answering, there must be certainty that such questions serve a useful purpose in assisting oneself and others towards 'It'.

You even quote Thomas Aquinas in his *Summa Theologiae*, to the effect that people are impeded from arriving at truth by (among other things) 'the great number of useless questions, arguments and articles'! And I recall that he laid aside the *Summa* eventually as 'straw' in comparison with the spiritual enlightenment that visited him before its end.

These qualifications have been in my own mind as I have set out on this whole project of receiving and responding to people's questions, and that is why I speak of 'responding' rather than 'answering'.

One of the differences between Buddhist spirituality and my own Christian growth is that a great deal of my spiritual life has been informed and energized by the basic teaching (doctrine or dogma) of the Christian faith. It is of supreme importance to me that God *is*, and that he has manifested his grace, mercy and love in the incarnation of Jesus as a human being, whose compassionate life and teaching is our pattern, and whose death and resurrection are the means of our forgiveness and life.

Having said that, in the context of Buddhist–Christian sharing, let me try to answer this question more directly. Over the years I have become increasingly aware of 'letting go' my intellectual imaging of the mystery of God. Christian doctrine has served as a kind of raft to carry me towards the other shore – that of participation in the divine life and love. But I have increasingly experienced the 'cloud of unknowing' in my ability to anticipate or describe what is happening to me. I can begin to speak of the results of being so 'moved upon', but I cannot describe what 'It' or the Godhead is in itself. Even writing these words makes me tremble! But there is a certain 'knowing', and that has enabled me to see (intuitively) the basic unity and interrelatedness of the cosmic network of being.

If any Christian readers are now frowning in perplexity, I would refer them to *A New Vision of Reality* by the Christian monk Bede Griffiths. A perceptive paragraph in his chapter 'Synthesis' indicates the dimension to which I am referring:

Every person and every thing is reintegrated into the One in a total unity transcending our present understanding. This is not, of course, something in time and space. It is an eternal and infinite reality and all of us even now are interwoven and interpenetrating in that one reality.[1]

As to my 'knowing' in relation to the cosmic order which involves animal life, I would say that I have been drawn into a contemplative awareness of my place in the moving pattern of the world so that the underlying unity is felt and experienced in my entering more deeply into myself. At the same time this is a reaching out along the pulsating web of life, and this causes me to consider my life as belonging to all other, and all other life to me.

Therefore, the sacredness of life has become a part of my personal and cosmic concern. It has brought me to a pacific stance in regard to my fellow creatures, expressed in reconciliation among humankind and my attitude as a brother to animal life. For me, whatever it may mean for others, I desire not to hurt other creatures and this has led me to become vegetarian. This is in accord with Buddhist practice – and many Christians are increasingly finding this to be an integral part of their spirituality.

There has been two-way traffic in this respect, for I still remember the powerful essay which Thomas Merton wrote during the Vietnam War, entitled 'Nhat Hanh is my brother',[2] affirming the bonds of solidarity and brotherhood in a worldwide contemplative vision. It is strange to recall that Merton died in 1968, while Thich Nhat Hanh continues to exercise a marvellous ecumenical ministry in Plum Village in France, teaching, writing, gardening and aiding refugees worldwide. The Hindu Ramakrishna Order was influenced by Christian social concern in its special blend of interior contemplation and humanitarian compassion. As we examine the roots of our spiritual traditions we find immense treasures, and these enable us to continue the process of cross-fertilization which is the joy of our sharing. Let me illustrate this by words from the seventh-century hermit, Isaac of Syria, which is a joyful response to this question:

> What is a compassionate heart? It is a heart on fire for the whole of creation, for humanity, for the birds, for the animals, for demons

and all that exists. At the recollection and at the sight of them such a person's eyes overflow with tears owing to the vehemence of the compassion which grips his heart; as a result of his deep mercy his heart shrinks and cannot bear to hear or look on any injury or the slightest suffering of anything in creation. This is why he constantly offers up prayer full of tears, even for the irrational animals and for the enemies of truth, even for those who harm him, so that they may be protected and find mercy. He even prays for the reptiles as a result of the great compassion which is poured out beyond measure – after the likeness of God – in his heart.[3]

This moving quotation brings to mind so many stories from my own Franciscan tradition flowing from the universal compassion of St Francis of Assisi. There are many similar stories from the Buddhist community.

Buddhists and Christians both belong to spiritual traditions in which there is a great deal to learn and a long way to go to attain the vision of the best of our prophets and contemplatives. In the future I believe that we shall recognize one another on the spiritual path, and help and encourage one another on the journey.

Reflection
As we think of our friendships across faith traditions, let us give thanks for the work of the divine Spirit in universal compassion, seeing ourselves as part of this cosmic network of sympathy and love.

26

Academic versus Spiritual

Q *In my theological training, there is an immense lack of balance. Spiritual and priestly formation is either taken for granted or left to chance, but by contrast the academic side is rigorous. Consequently, you get priests who can tell you the difference an iota makes to homos in the Greek text, with its implications*

– but who may not be capable of practical empathy and compassion in their parishes (and I don't exclude myself!). Am I right in thinking that this is a worrying imbalance, and that things should change? (Louis)

R It sounds to me, Louis, as if your particular theological college needs a good shaking up! I would be the first to affirm with Carlyle that Christendom stands or falls by the difference an *iota* makes (as you know, it has bearing on the matter of whether the Christ is of the *same* Being or simply *similar* to the Father). But of what use is academic or dogmatic truth without the dimension of spirituality and the life of prayer and compassion in the training of a priest in the Church of God? I'm sure that Thomas the disciple would have been amazed (or possibly not interested!) if the '*iota* controversy' had been presented to him when he fell down before the risen Christ, crying: 'My Lord and my God!' (John 20.28).

I know that what you say is true in some areas of theological training, but I am impressed by the quality and enthusiasm of ordinands (men and women) who come or write to me from different parts of the Church and with various spiritual traditions. The whole area of spirituality has opened up amazingly in the last two decades, and one is as likely to be exposed to Ignatian spirituality in a Baptist College as to encounter charismatic gifts and graces in a Roman Catholic seminary. There is a great mingling of denominations training together with the cross-fertilization that this encourages. A Free Church ordinand made his confession at my hermitage recently, and a Quaker receives communion at Glasshampton when he comes on retreat.

Your particular college may be trailing behind, but it encourages me immensely to find the spiritual depth which is found in the spirituality courses at the evangelical London Bible College on the one hand and at the traditionally Catholic College of the Resurrection at Mirfield. I am not at all discouraged by the lively reciprocal debates which are part of theological training these days, so I would encourage you not only to persevere, but to get a Franciscan friar, a Catholic Jesuit and staff members from Spurgeon's College, London Bible College and St John's, Nottingham to share their experience with your staff and students. This morning I had a warm letter from one of the seminarians at the Catholic seminary in Guildford, enthusiastic about the content of his ordination training, and affirming love and fellowship in Christ.

It is essential that spiritual formation is in the forefront of pastoral training, for if the shepherds are not trained in mind and heart for their pastoral task, where will the sheep turn?

Reflection

If you are involved in theological training at any level why not write to the main-line theological colleges asking for their prospectus with details of pastoral spirituality courses (don't forget return postage!). This will not only give you (and your peer group) information across the denominational board, but will enable you to see how contemporary theological training spills over to lay folk. 'Doing theology' will then more clearly be seen as the task of all the people of God.

27

Jazz and Quaker Silence

Q *I am a Quaker and much appreciate the place of communal silence. I have also spent many years as a trumpet player in the jazz and big band scene. Do you find this contradictory, as some Christians seem to? (Denny)*

R This is a bit mischievous, Denny – you ask this question knowing that I have recently written to you in appreciation of your Duke Ellington *Sacred Concert* recordings, and that great Duke cassette *Ring dem Bells!*

Perhaps our non-talking meals would be enriched by the Jacques Loussier Jazz Trio playing Bach and Vivaldi. I've listened, this morning, to his treatment of Bach's *Air on a G String*, and I realize that we would have to make quite clear to the retreatants what they were in for.

Having said all that, one of my most joyous experiences was when I celebrated a Mozart Mass in the baroque church at Witley Court, with a small orchestra and choir, and with celebrant, deacon and sub-deacon in medieval vestments. In the brief homily I reminded the congregation that the Swiss theologian Karl Barth played an hour of Mozart every morning before beginning work on his *magnum opus*, *Church Dogmatics*.

No one who has shared in the Bach *St Matthew Passion* at the Royal Festival Hall during Holy Week can doubt the power of that portrayal of the passion of Christ in holy words and sublime music. Yet we should remember that his haunting Passion Chorale, 'O Sacred Head', was based on the melody of a popular street song of the day.

Can you imagine a recording of simple and polyphonic plainchant, over which a jazz saxophonist improvises a soaring descant within the acoustic beauty of a monastic chapel? That is a description of *Officium* by the Hilliard Ensemble, a vocal quartet, with Jan Garbarek and his soprano and tenor saxophones.[1] There are 15 mind-blowing tracks which, for me, evoke a haunting and numinous beauty in a human adoration of the divine. I would be curious to know Duke Ellington's or Count Basie's response!

It is clear, however, that God's people are far less tolerant and open-minded than their Lord, but things are changing. I recall that when Duke Ellington's Sacred Jazz Concert, which began at the Cathedral of St John the Divine in New York, and travelled to the Church of St Sulpice, Paris, Coventry Cathedral, and then to the Church of Santa Maria del Mar in Barcelona, the attendance and appreciation was intoxicating. In Barcelona the congregation burst into the aisles to participate in the finale, 'Praise God and Dance'. And they did! The Duke died in 1974, and over 10,000 people attended his funeral, and this bears its own witness to his kind of music and spirituality.[2]

The wonderful thing is to be able to combine an obvious enjoyment and participation in the jazz scene with the worship and meditation tradition of Quaker silence. These are days in which some of the old musical categories are breaking down, and it is evident that God communicates with us in the experience of a wide spectrum of music – from Gregorian plainsong to jazz!

I think of all this today, as you sit in Quaker silence, and I sit on the prayer stool in my hermitage.

Reflection

Here is a good quotation for a Quaker, and one which should make all Christians reflect in silence, from George Steiner:

Music puts our being as men and women in touch with that which transcends the sayable, and which outstrips the analysable . . . It has long been, and continues to be, the unwritten theology of those who lack or reject any formal creed.[3]

28

Dangerous Praying

Q *Do you think that it is possible to pray for someone constantly, even over a long period, and for the prayer 'not to work' because the one prayed for is raising a barrier, through fear or cynicism, and therefore effectively chooses not to be helped? (Pearl)*

R When I read this question, I immediately thought of those remarkable verses in Mark's Gospel:

And Jesus could do no deed of power there, except that he laid his hands on a few sick people and cured them. And he was amazed at their unbelief (6.5–6).

I am amazed that human unbelief could restrain the power of God, and that there are those who will not allow the healing power of Christ into their broken lives.

This is the sort of question in which I need to know *who* is asking, and what kind of person he or she is. I know you as a capable, professional and intelligent woman, Pearl – a committed Christian with a profound sensitivity to others, psychically aware of the joys and pains of those with whom you are in relationship.

Prayer is vital, but you must be aware of how potentially dangerous it is to lay yourself open to spiritual powers. You see, it is possible to engage in communion not only with light, life and truth, but also with darkness and evil. The Christian is guarded by baptism and confession of the lordship of Christ, but needs also to take heed of St Paul's counsel to be armed and armoured against the powers of darkness with which we wrestle in the spiritual realms (Ephesians 6.10–20).

If people realized that they can be in touch with spiritual powers and realities which are dark and evil as well as with the love and power of God, they would be more aware in their praying, and more careful to take the name of Christ into their minds and hearts as they begin the adventure of prayer, and especially as they intercede for themselves and for others. Prayer can be dangerous!

I am a little apprehensive about the wording of this question because it sounds as if you are engaging in a technique that 'works' or not, and that sounds as if it is a matter of psychical or mechanistic control over the object of your prayers. I'm sure you don't mean it like that; in intercessory prayer believers are laying themselves open to the healing power of God in Christ, so that the Holy Spirit can pray in and through them, to the alleviation of pain and suffering, and for the greater good of the person prayed for – whether that be salvation, healing or guidance.

Then from the other person's side, it is not that they are faced with someone who says: 'I'm praying for you and am determined that you will be influenced and changed!' If that were the case, you couldn't blame the person for saying: 'I'm certainly not going to be manipulated by your desires or prayers!' – and that would be putting up an effective barrier.

Your prayer for that person should rather seek the loving will of God for them, not trying to brandish your spiritual weapons as a threat, or even in expressed pity or condolence or judgement of them. It is a matter of loving intercession in the secret place.

The Holy Spirit will not manipulate, but lead the person to understand that their greatest good and deepest peace is in the life of love. This will be in God's time, at God's pace and in God's way. We can pray, but we must leave the results with God. Indeed, our involvement in prayer will change our own attitude, and make us gentle, understanding and less threatening – thus we may be used by God in answering our own prayers.

So, yes, people can resist, for good and bad reasons. But if our prayers are lovingly directed and according to the will of God, then we shall be protected from dark powers, and love will grow in our hearts and in the lives of those for whom we pray.

Reflection

If we compare Paul's prayer for the believers in Ephesians 1.15–23, with his counsel for intercessors in Ephesians 6.10–20, we can examine our motives in praying, and our concern for God's will to be done in and through those for whom we pray. We should then ask ourselves if our attitude has changed over the period of our intercession. The answer will indicate whether our prayers are on course!

29

Protesting and Proselytizing

Q *My husband and I are both committed Christians. Our daughter (in her twenties) is an environmental protester and recently spent two weeks in Holloway Prison for her part in the Newbury protest, shocking us both. Our son is involved in mission work for the conversion of Muslims. From both sides we feel challenged and wonder what commitment and discipleship mean? (Joan)*

R Thank you, Joan, for your fuller letter telling me the story of your daughter's integrity and your son's evangelical zeal. I admire both, and am not sorry that you are shocked by their very different attitudes and behaviour, for good can come out of it. There are times when Christians must stand against the state, and times when they must stand in bold witness for Christ. But – and this is a big but – you have to sort out what is Christ's will, and what is simply the expression of your own (perhaps misguided) zeal and stubbornness.

I see your dilemma, though. You have never before been personally involved in civil disobedience which has involved a prison sentence, and your daughter was convinced that the Newbury bypass was a case in which she felt a moral obligation to protest – and prison was the result. You are also a Christian who feels that she should not persuade others to convert from their own faith – and now your son is on a mission to do that very thing. It is not simply a matter of courage in either case, but

71

whether such behaviour is right. Let me share a piece of my own experience.

I hold pacifist convictions, and as a young Christian, believing military service to be morally wrong, had to face a tribunal, and indicated my willingness to go to prison for my convictions. I still believe I was right and sincere, and I would do it again. But I do have fellowship with Christians who are not pacifists and who present me with equally sincere and difficult alternatives.

Also, I believe in sharing the good news of Christ, the saviour of the world, with enthusiasm and zeal. But I do not waylay and confront Buddhist or Hindu friends with exclusivist claims. Rather, I listen to the good things they have to say (and Christians can learn a good deal from other traditions), and share with them my understanding of Christ as Saviour and redeemer. I don't water down the gospel of Christ, but I know what it is to be aggressively evangelized by missionary groups.

The issues are too big to discuss here, for they involve theological, social and political problems, including questions of violence in areas of civil disobedience and international evangelism. In my own case I am guided by gospel principles. These indicate that I should always stand firmly for truth, with the willingness to suffer the consequences. But I should do this lovingly and non-violently, with an openness to all people of good will.

Commitment to Christ means to believe and behave in a Christ-like way, and discipleship means that the follower radiates the healing love of the saviour in all circumstances. Nevertheless that means standing against all that is unjust and savours of hatred and cruelty. Such a stand evokes plenty of reaction!

Reflection

If we have loved ones and friends whose positive attitudes and obvious integrity challenge, perplex and distress us, we should be willing to provide a space for them to talk, pray and discuss. Fervent zeal may need to be tempered by mature wisdom; cool indifference may need to be fired by enthusiasm. If the outcome is continuing disagreement in certain areas, then let it be in loving support, where this is possible, but always with mutual desire to know the mind of Christ.

30

Charismatic Confusion

Q *I have been involved in many supernatural healing meetings where emotion has run high and people have been supposedly touched by God. Can you understand why now, looking back, I just feel cheapened and used by the whole experience, and want nothing more to do with these healing and blessing revival meetings?* (Mervyn)

R Yes, Mervyn, I see that you are describing situations and experiences which have wounded, hurt and perplexed you. My first response is to hold you in sympathy, to allow you to share the whole burden of pain with me, including the tears, so that we can be open to the healing Christ who is the great physician.

What you have described – and some aspects of what has been called 'the Toronto blessing' – have been counterproductive, and have driven some people away from an evaluation of what is good and wholesome in the charismatic movement. I don't want you now to act negatively against all things charismatic, for both the classic Pentecostal movement and the charismatic movement, which have affected all the mainline Churches, have brought much renewal and blessing.

In this situation, as in most situations which involve controversial doctrine or practice, there is a middle way which is not a way of compromise, but of spiritual discernment and maturity. God does sometimes work in miraculous ways, and there are gifts of healing as well as prophetic and charismatic ministries in the Church – but they do not always reside among those who make the most noise or claim supernatural gifts. There are also great dangers – such as maintaining that if physical healing is not experienced, then it is due to lack of faith, or that if you tithe your money or property, then in a 'pact of plenty' God is obliged to increase your prosperity!

Hankering after supernatural gifts and graces is a sign of immaturity, and the mystical tradition evaluates many charismatic manifestations as spiritual adolescence which should be left behind as one progresses in the life of prayer. The way of Christ is more surely manifested in simplicity of life, giving away the superfluous and living in compassion. Christ is often found among those who are incapacitated physically and mentally, and among the terminally ill.

Your journey has caused you to move out of the charismatic movement and to share worship among those whose expression is more liturgical and contemplative. This may be necessary for your wounds to heal and for your spiritual equilibrium to be restored. But then your task will be the discovery of a pattern which allows for the whole spectrum of liturgical, contemplative and charismatic worship in the Church of God, reflecting temperamental, national, denominational, traditional and theological diversity – but all within the unity of the body of Christ.

Reflection

If we have been wounded and hurt in our fellowship with the people of God, we must look to Christ as the great physician, and then, experiencing his healing power, seek to bind up the wounds of others who suffer from the bigotry and insensitivities of others. In this way we can become channels of healing for the reconciling Christ.

31

Prayer and Demanding Children

Q *When I was single and fairly independent I had time to develop a prayer life, though I must admit I didn't use the time wisely. But now, four years into marriage, with two young children, and with both of us involved in professional work, we find ourselves exhausted. How can we begin praying seriously, let alone maintain a firm and disciplined prayer life with so many demands – especially children? (Jayne)*

R When you write about the joy your children give you, Jayne, and when I think of the letters and conversations I have with 'young marrieds' (most of whom I've known since their single days), the more I wonder why they come to me with their problems in prayer. I think, perhaps, I should be going to them. A friend, David, who is on the staff of a theological college, wrote recently and raised a similar question to yours. And a month or so later he wrote again, and in the last paragraph of his letter was this beautiful experience concerning his three-year-old Joshua:

> The night before the new term started found me lying awake in Joshua's bed. After calming him out of a restless dream, the familiar mixture of snuffles, grunts and kicks led him again to the place that children call sleep. But I lay there, wide awake, crushed under the weight of a thousand trivial concerns on the edge of a new job.
>
> A tiny hand reached out in the dark and patted me twice on the head: 'It's all right, Daddy', he said. The word was confirmed with signs following – as he shoved his finger up my nose. I turned to him, eyes moist with gratitude (and pain), but he was deep in his dreams. 'Out of the mouths of babes and infants . . .'

There is a lesson in prayer. Of course, I do have some things to recommend, listening to your specific problems and commending to you methods of meditation and contemplative prayer both ancient and new. But in the last analysis you have to begin where you are – pray as you can and not as you can't.

Touch, look, listen and enter into the world of your children, from birth, through infancy, into childhood. Let the children's world be the place where you learn absolute trust, spontaneity, abandoned expression of needs, a sense of wonder, of creativity, of experiment and curiosity.

Some years ago I visited a Christian potter friend whose wife was Hindu. Before we retired to the pottery for a lesson on throwing a pot, we went as a family to their meditation room. Their little four-year-old boy came with us. He sat cross-legged, with a *shrutti* box (concertina for chanting), and after an 'Om' chant and a song, 'Jesus, how lovely you are', we remained in silence. Little Emrys was a model of quietness and stillness, and he was certainly centred – more than we were!

Buddhist friends tell me that they teach their children meditation as soon as they are able to sit upright, sitting in formal meditation from two and a half years old – with even dog and cat sitting too!

So read and practise the kind of methods of prayer and meditation I advocate, but let your primary concern be with the care of your children at this point in your life. Doubtless you will have experiences like David's, and you will stimulate in me (who have no children) a godly envy for such insights into prayer, trust and love.

Reflection

Let us ask the Lord to lead us into the children's world, touching, watching, listening, so that we may become childlike in our joyful and spontaneous dependence upon God.

32

God in the Present Moment

Q *In the kitchen at Glasshampton there is (or was) a poster saying: 'Those who sing pray twice over'. Isn't spirituality more a matter of attitude than of practice? (Alan)*

R The poster has disappeared, Alan, but the sentiment (from St Augustine) holds good. His point was that words wedded to music offer twofold praise to God, both in the words and the music. Your point seems to be that work is its own prayer, so why do we need to say prayers?

I think it is not a matter of working *or* praying, but of finding the reality and joy of God's loving presence in all we do, in all we say, in all we are. God's being is mediated to us at different levels and at different stages of our lives, and there is nothing (apart from sin) that cannot be an instrument of his love.

To some people it is evident that communion with God is primarily found in prayer, Scripture, sacraments and worship – though it is interesting that some of the early Franciscans and mystics, like the thirteenth-century Richard Rolle, found God more intimately outside religious services – in the fields and woods, under the canopy of the sky.

Of course, we do not all find God in all things – some of us may be colour-blind or tone-deaf, so art and music would not then be the place of God's revelation to us (at least in this life). But God is to be found in the common and ordinary things as well as in the mind-blowing or mystical experiences which elevate our spirits to dimensions of vision or ecstasy.

When Brother Lawrence was 18 years old he received a moment of revelation in the simple observation of a tree in full bloom. This carried him into his monastic vocation, and after some years of practising the presence of God, he could say:

> The time of business with me does not differ from the time of prayer; and in the noise and clatter of my kitchen, while several persons are at the same time calling for different things, I possess God in as great tranquillity as if I were upon my knees at the blessed sacrament.[1]

Some people have called this 'the sacrament of the present moment', finding God in everything, at any time, and especially mindfully in where I am now, in what I am doing now, in this place. One of my favourite sayings of St Francis is this:

> Wherever we are, wherever we go, we bring our cell with us. Our brother body is our cell and our soul is the hermit living in that cell in order to pray to God and meditate. If our soul does not live in peace and solitude within its cell, of what avail is it to live in a man-made cell?[2]

This is another way of saying with St Paul: 'Your body is a temple of the Holy Spirit within you' (1 Corinthians 6.19), so that all five senses, all powers of intellect and mind, and all movements of creative love and spiritual understanding – all these are channels of the divine energy and the divine mercy. Therefore singing and praying, living and working, creating and loving, alone and in fellowship with others – all are places where the divine and human meet in joy.

Reflection

Let us seek today to exercise our intuitive faculties – sensing the presence of God in what we encounter in people and places, and responding to that presence in joy and openness.

33

Harassing God

Q *Thinking of the 'Friend at Midnight' parable (Luke 11.5–8), is God more likely to answer our request if it is prayed ceaselessly, and if we get someone else – or 100 people – to join with us, rather than if we prayed alone? (Pauline)*

R Yes, Pauline, I see your problem! I am imagining hundreds of prayer-wheels turning, 24-hour barrages of prayer warriors, and universal sponsored pray-ins to get a reluctant God to take notice! I'm indulging in a bit of levity because you can push parables over the edge of meaning, pressing them towards illogical and erroneous ends. It is good for us to make our requests known to God, not to give up when times are dark, and to share the ministry of petition and intercession with the people of God. But God already loves us, knows the longings and desires of our hearts, and does not need armies of belligerent petitioners to harass him until he takes notice. Such a scenario is more like the prophets of Baal than the people of God (see 1 Kings 18.26–9).

Yet some Christians question the very possibility of petitionary and intercessionary prayer, and after years of 'shopping-list prayer', give up because they are not persuaded of its efficacy and question its theology.

Prayer is communion with God, and this is much wider and deeper than petition or intercession. Through my writings I have spent many years in leading Evangelical and Catholic Christians into the profound wonder and mystery of contemplative prayer. But I do not therefore neglect prayers of petition and intercession – though I do now understand them in a different way.

When I ask people to pray for or with me, or when people ask me to pray for them, I enter into a network of compassion. I yield myself to God in order that the Holy Spirit may groan and cry, weep and worship in and through me – expressing the healing will of God. It is as though I were the flute through which the Holy Spirit breathes, creating melodies of intercession.

The saving, reconciling energies of God flow along this creative network of compassion, communicating healing love among warring nations, deprived and tortured people, and bringing hope into the lives of helpless, terminally ill folk. These energies work towards the alleviation of suffering, towards deliverance, or a good and gentle death.

So no prayer is individualistic, though it may be intensely personal. We are all in it together, and our prayer is the prayer of the cosmic Christ. All true prayer is offered within the communion of saints. If it is 'in the Spirit' (that is, linked with this network of compassion), then it contributes towards the increase of hope, light and love in the world.

So, if prayer is viewed in this cosmic manner, and as part of the ongoing prayer of Christ to the Father, it becomes universal, part of the whole contemplative venture, and is one with the healing energies of God in nature and within humanity as a whole.

So get thinking and get praying at a more profound level, and with all the saints!

Reflection

Perhaps we need to be delivered from mechanical or cajoling ways of praying. We need to live and pray in the Holy Spirit, so that our lives may be taken up into the river of intercession which leads to the ocean of God's love.

PART THREE

Questions of Practice

34

Open-Minded or Compromising?

Q *Some Christian friends have a narrow and dogmatic outlook, and they will not have fellowship with those who differ from them in their own faith, and cannot relate at all to those of other faiths. How open can one be without compromise?* (Myfanwy)

R This is a thorny subject, Myfanwy, especially if you have friends who are both to the left and right of your own position. I have some friends who question the salvation of most Roman Catholics (and certainly of the pope!), of many Anglicans, and of many in the mainstream denominations. But I have other friends who have watered down the gospel in such a reductionist way that it ceases to be Christian. You see, we all have our sticking-points, and we place our lines of demarcation in different places. After all, those friends you refer to could say that the way is narrow (Matthew 7.13–14), that they must be dogmatic because dogma means doctrine and we must avoid false doctrine (2 Timothy 4.3–5). Of course, they will interpret how narrow the way should be and what the false doctrine is – but then, so do we!

Clearly we cannot refuse to eat with members of our family or our friends who do not accept the gospel, nor can we bar them from our homes (2 John 10). Nor should we consign anyone to Satan for the destruction of their body so that their soul shall be saved (1 Corinthians 5.5). Yet these practices were found in the early Church, and because of that, they are still practised by sect-groups on the edge of today's Church. And this in spite of the fact that Jesus ate with publicans and sinners, and was friendly and compassionate towards adulterers.

I have always had a wide spectrum of Christian friends, but many of them, in my early days, would not have dreamed of relating to a

Buddhist, Sikh or Hindu, even if there had been opportunity. There was even great caution in being friendly to a Jew, unless you witnessed to Christ as Messiah! What I did find especially suspect (recognizing it as spiritual blackmail) was the encouraging of friendliness to non-Christians in order to win them to Christ!

Some of my friends were so conservative they believed in 'guarding' their pulpit and the holy communion, lest someone should deviate from *their* interpretation of the Bible or receive communion while not in *their* fellowship.

I find it all so fantastic now, and certainly found it counterproductive then, for I reacted against it. And yet, although I rejoice in the openness and freedom which I practise among all the people of God now, I know there were many sincere and devoted people among the fundamentalists I've mentioned. If you ever belonged to such a group, you will know how much courage it takes to stand against the party-line, and how difficult it is to break away from such religious bondage.

But where does all this leave us? Well, sometimes we have to be pastorally right even if we are theologically wrong! So I would encourage you to be open and loving in all your relationships, while not swallowing a vacuous theology which is neither Catholic nor Evangelical. There are stands to be made, both theologically and morally, and while we may be compassionate in all our dealings, we should not be shoddy and inconsistent when the issues are serious.

You will see through this book that I believe that the light of the hidden Christ, or Logos, may be found in the lives and teachings of our Hindu brother or our Sikh and Buddhist sister. These are days of dialogue and genuine sharing, so that two-way traffic is encouraged and no one is keeping a points score!

Keep all your friends on board if you can – introduce them to each other, and that will put the cat among the pigeons (or the sheep among the goats). I don't want to be flippant, but sometimes Jesus shows us a more loving, joyous, disciplined and humorous pattern than many of his servants!

Reflection

I remember the story of Moses, the Desert Father, who, when he was called into the community meeting to judge and condemn a brother, eventually came carrying a basket full of holes from which sand was running out behind him. 'I come to condemn a brother', he said, 'and my own sins are running out like sand.'

35

Compassion Fatigue

Q *I've always felt it is not enough to believe the creed and receive the sacraments of the Church – we should also put into practice the teaching of Jesus in our social lives. This has led me to support financially and practically agencies which work for equality and justice. But over the last year or two I have become increasingly angry, helpless and frustrated with issues in which human beings never seem to learn. I even find my anger levelled at victims of oppression – though I thought I was a sympathetic Christian. What are your comments on this? (Patricia)*

R You'll see I've chosen the heading 'Compassion Fatigue' for your question, Patricia, because it fits your description. There comes a time, especially when we expend more energy and time than we replace, when we get tired and irritable. If nothing is done about it, we get impatient with those who never learn, and perhaps we see our money, energies, sympathy and hard work disappear into a black hole of fathomless human and ecological need – and it is never enough.

The result of all this, if action is not taken, is that the feeling of helplessness increases, anger and impatience-levels rise, and we bring things to a head in a temperamental explosion or have some kind of breakdown. It is possible for the breakdown to take the form of a purely negative mental and emotional retreat from the battle lines, and we may become paralysed in other areas of our lives.

A great deal of the problem is a contemporary one. We are confronted daily, hourly, even moment by moment, with each new international crisis as it arises, via the various media. A plane crashes killing 200 people; there is another intertribal massacre in Rwanda or Burundi; an earthquake kills many innocent people; an oppressive regime maims, kills and tortures its own people using arms purchased from Britain, France and the USA. As the morning paper falls through the letterbox, we are faced with yet another starving or maimed child, or with victims of famine and abuse, and we erupt and cry out that we don't want to see another picture of such horrific and savage cruelty.

Many of these things have happened previously, but we were not constantly faced with them, nor did we feel that we *had* to watch them, know about them, confront them and even feel responsible for them.

Let me tell you how I deal with this, remembering that we are all temperamentally different, and have different gifts and vocations. At least it will give you a few principles to guide your thinking. You know that I am now exploring the hermit life with no TV, though I do listen to the news and have a weekly scan of a responsible newspaper to inform my intercessions and ministry.

When I was out and about as a parish priest, university chaplain, and later as a friar in the Society of St Francis, I came to conclusions about myself and the world's need. I have never been a party-political animal, so I had to decide where my energies should be channelled in issues of social concern, justice and peace. I had many sympathies (peace issues, animal rights, green/ecological concerns), but I knew that if I went preaching on my soap-box, marching with protesters, influencing others by writing and preaching on the increasing number of relevant issues, I would dissipate my energies, drive my friends mad and run myself into the ground – for I am an enthusiast, and like to make my stance clear!

So I sorted out my priorities after looking at the issues I felt I could influence, prayed the matter through, and contributed money, time and talents to Amnesty International. There were times when other issues took my attention, but I put most of my eggs into the one basket, and left the rest to others. I realized that I did not have an infinite fund of compassion, and could only deal with a small share of the world's ills, but I took on *my* share, and in so doing felt linked into that interrelated web of compassion in which all people of good will are involved.

There was an element of realistic humour involved too, for I was (and am) reminded that I am neither powerfully influential or indispensable, so I could laugh at my own posturing and yet realize that I had my part to play in my small corner.

Of course, when I answered the call to explore the hermit life, I even had to let go those areas of responsible care – but again, I was entering into a profounder knowledge of myself and my place in the nature of things, and that was within the wider will of God.

Actually, I seem to have more influence on more people from my hermitage, though that is not the reason I am living this life. The point I am making is that if you find out *your* place in the scheme of things, then more will be accomplished in and through you as an instrument of God's grace.

These principles, together with a disciplined life of prayer and meditation (essential!), will bring you to a place of balance, of rest, of letting go all those frenetic activities in which *you* worked for God, and instead allowing him to show you how *he* can work in and through you.

Letting go is a primary task. Resign from committees, stop fundraising, lay aside all the heart-rending literature, stop marching, protesting, organizing and picketing. Let it all go and take a sabbatical – for unless you do, you will become a burden instead of a blessing, and it will all turn counterproductive before you have your breakdown, or meltdown, or whatever the present jargon is.

Then, from that place of quietness and rest, let something arise from within you, in God's time and in God's way. You will probably need help to do this – perhaps a good parish priest, soul friend or counsellor. You don't have to initiate but to respond, not to move mountains but be moved by the Spirit. And the 'new thing' which will come into being may be simple and modest, but it will be more effective, enhancing your own life as well as the cause which comes to hand and heart.

Reflection

None of us is either indispensable or invincible! We must take ourselves seriously with good humour, and be open, pliable and responsible to what the Holy Spirit is saying within us.

36

Don't Take it too Heavy!

Q *I've always felt sensitive and concerned about the world's problems and suffering, and over the past few years have felt pulled down by them all. Over the last weeks I have had a series of physical symptoms beginning with chest pains, dizziness and vomiting. After hospital tests I have been told I have no cardiac or other recognizable problems, but I continue to feel weak and a bit afraid. I can feel the links with my anxieties about the state of the world, and wonder if you have anything to say that might help? (Neil)*

R Some years ago, Neil, I had a priest friend who used to come to me for counselling. One of his problems was that he read the newspapers, and was fed a constant diet of violence, atrocities, massacres and insoluble international conflicts on TV, and he had begun to feel that they were sucking him into levels of depression and that somehow he was responsible for some of it. His helplessness in the situation was making matters worse.

It has taken him some years to break free of this cycle of anxiety and guilt, and he has had to look deeper into his own past life to find some of the reasons for his psychic frailty, and this question reminds me of him.

One of the contemporary problems is the instant communication we are subjected to in our society. Not only is there an on-the-spot reporter and TV crew, but the last bit of gore and violence is wrung out of each situation. I must say that I am glad I do not have TV in my hermitage!

We cannot close our eyes to the world's ills – indeed, we must be involved in issues of peace and justice, and in the alleviation of pain and suffering. But we cannot take upon our individual souls the whole burden of the world, and the heavy information load does not help us to avoid doing so!

I think of Rabbi Lionel Blue as a deeply sensitive and gentle soul, who often uses his humour to keep a certain objective and healthy distance from the wrong kind of involvement in anxiety and guilt, saying: 'Don't take it too heavy' – and I think his attitude and his words are sound. He could not be accused of ghetto-like retreat from moral issues and respon-sibilities, but he knows that he is capable of only so much compassion and so much action.

I know how deeply people feel, for example, about ecological imbalance and pollution due to human abuse and greed. We all bear our share of responsibility for it and have to acknowledge that and play our part personally and politically to ameliorate the situation. But I also believe that we must realize that one of our problems can be taking it all too much to heart and too personally. After all, as individuals, we are not wholly responsible for the destruction of the rain forests or the thinning of the ozone layer! We sometimes need to get things in perspective, even laugh at our own sense of importance, put our heads together with a trusted counsellor and work out our immediate concerns.

It seems to me that if we are to be a help and not a burden, we must look to our own physical and psychical health, not take the whole gamut of abuses on ourselves, but simply sort out one or perhaps two areas where we can contribute modestly, and then through prayer and meditation, get our spiritual balance right, thus going forward gently. 'Don't take it too heavy', but let us lift up our hearts, for the world's suffering and redemption are ultimately in the hands of God.

Reflection

We must realize that when we give attention to our personal needs of body, mind and spirit, we are thereby better equipped to give objective sympathy and help to those around us. A sense of modest perspective is necessary for our mature response.

37

Organ Transplants – Gift or Presumption?

Q *What place do organ transplants have? Are they 'the ultimate gift of life from the death of others', or does such surgery contradict the will of God? (Alistair)*

R As a GP, Alistair, you must have encountered both these extreme views. When the South African surgeon Christian Barnard performed the first heart transplants in the 1960s, there was acclaim and apprehension at such radical transplantation of a vital organ.

There have been so many innovations which were first of all greeted with fear or caution and have later been found to save and enrich human life, so we must not rush to conclusions. But these days we find ourselves surrounded by new areas of experimentation and medical and genetic possibility, and this causes us to ask moral and ethical questions which have not previously been asked. After all, it is one thing to receive the heart of another human being, but what if it was suggested to you that the transplantation was to be of a pig's heart?

I have a number of friends who are apprehensive and cautious about the whole matter of transplantation of vital organs, and others who have had such surgery and have been given an extra decade or more of life. In the last analysis, it must be a matter of personal and conscientious thought, helped by trusted and medical friends.

Caution is necessary because of mistakes and abuses – the transfusion of HIV-infected blood was a scandal in France, and as I write these words, today's news tells of a number of British patients who have received corneal grafts from a donor who died from the horrific Creutzfeld Jacob's disease, though the receiving hospital was not told of this fact!

But lest we make accidents and abuses the reason for not allowing medical progress, it is well for us to recall the positive blessings that transplant surgery has brought to so many. There is a remarkable story told by Morris West in his novel *Lazarus*. In it the future Pope Leo XIV needs radical cardiac surgery. In a perceptive and powerful interview with his Jewish surgeon Salviati, he is told of the necessary surgery and prognosis, and given counsel about his attitude. The book is worth reading as a salutary comment on our mortal finitude, and the extract worth quoting:

> You will be unconscious for at least forty-eight hours, perfused with potent anaesthetics. You will continue to be fed opiates and analgesics until the discomforts are within tolerable limits. However, you will suffer something else: a psychic trauma, a personality change whose dimensions still elude full explanation. You will be emotionally fragile – as prone to tears as to rage. You will be subject to depressions, sudden, black and sometimes suicidal. At one moment you will be as dependent as a child, seeking reassurance after a nightmare. The next you will be angry and frustrated by your own impotence. Your short-term memory may be defective. Your tolerance of emotional stress will be greatly reduced. You will be strongly advised by the counsellors who will be working with you not to make any important decisions, emotional, intellectual or administrative, for at least three months . . . Most of these sequelae will pass. Some will remain, diminished but always present in your psychic life. The better your physical condition the less will be your emotional handicap. So, after the first period of convalescence, you will be put on a rigid diet to lose fifteen or twenty kilograms. You will be required to do daily exercise on a graduated scale. And if you fail to do either of those things your psychic handicap will continue, and your physical condition will deteriorate rapidly. In short, the whole exercise will be a painful futility. I'm sorry to make such a huge mouthful of this, but it is absolutely necessary that you understand it. Believe me, I do not exaggerate.[1]

We live in a country where there are still high standards of medical care and research, despite immense financial problems and revolutionary NHS shake-ups and changes. But we must be on the alert in the whole area of legitimate and illegitimate research, pressing for the setting up of a council of medical ethics, consisting of BMA, medical research, religious, philosophical and humanist input which has objectively free status. Such a body, with occasional co-opted experts, could take on board the ethical, religious and philosophical implications of whole areas of potential research, including genetic engineering, and should be able to act as a mediating interpreter to the public. There may be a publication including debate and occasional papers, perhaps an ongoing journal. If only GPs weren't so worked off their feet, perhaps some of them could be seconded to act in this mediating kind of way.

Reflection

If the reader is in any way involved in areas where religion and medicine work together, make a list of the university and medical departments and boards which are concerned with ethics in medicine, making it available to local GPs and churches. Your own church fellowship may profit by information, involvement and prayer in these areas where religion and medicine overlap.

38

Admiring yet Agnostic

Q *My father and I have debates over the Christian faith. He says he is an agnostic, but has great regard for the teaching of Jesus. Yet always he asks why God allows little children to suffer. Should I keep trying? (Morris)*

R Your question paints a picture, Morris. Obviously there is a measure of openness between you both or you wouldn't go on talking – but I wonder whether this is not your question as well as his?

Let me suppose that you, like us all, are struggling with the problem of suffering which I have spoken of elsewhere (see Chapters 56 and 57), but that you still are persuaded that God is a loving creator and redeemer who desires you to live in sympathy and compassion. If your father sees his married son managing his family well and following a way of life in which Christ is Saviour and example, he must be impressed. Perhaps this is why he is an agnostic and not an atheist!

If you look at my response in Chapters 56 and 57, you will realize that I respect someone who says 'I don't know', rather than someone who dogmatically asserts that there is no God, no loving purpose and no meaning to life apart from the meaning that we bring to it. This is a sorry existence, but there are some sincere people who come to that conclusion. The 'don't know' of the agnostic is open to the mysteries of life which come to us from all things true, good and beautiful, and the agnostic is also open to persuasion – but I suggest that the persuasion does not lie in debate but in friendship, example and private prayer. Be ready to share with him if and when the questions come up, or if reading material can be recommended – but realize that he is already half way there!

Of course there are 'don't knows' who don't want to know. But there are also 'don't knows' who would very much like to know. And this matter of 'knowing' is a knowledge of faith. It is not like a chemical or mathematical formula which can be proven beyond doubt. Yet there are experiments which can be carried out. Let me tell you about one.

A fellow in his 30s came to Glasshampton and told me that he had found one of my books, looked through it, and decided to come for a few days to explore. He said he had not believed in God, that his business life was prospering, but his personal life was empty, and was throwing up questions of meaning that he could not answer. I suggested to him that he went through brief sections of the book he had been reading, adding to it parts of Mark's Gospel, and that he went walking each day he was here, acting as if it were true.

He did this as an experiment, and at the end of it said: 'I told you that I had never had a religious experience in my life before. I can no longer say that.' We began there. That was over ten years ago, and he continues to grow in the path of Christian prayer and discipleship.

Not all people have such dramatic stories of discovery – there are others in my own experience who continue friendship with me and continue in a certain agnosticism. But I do not get over-anxious about them, but quietly live, pray, work, share with them. And because they are open, honest and genuine, I expect them, ultimately, to find, or rather be found by, the Lord. Of course, I do not know whether that will be in this life – but it doesn't end there. This means that we do not need to become destructively anxious and obsessively argumentative in terms of the agnosticism of our friends and family members, for ultimately we are all in the hands of a tender and understanding saviour who will not let us go.

Reflection

Why not bring an enquiring agnostic friend on retreat to Glasshampton or elsewhere? You could both use the time as suits you – with a bit of walking and working included, and sharing in as much or as little of the chapel life as you liked. And if you wanted a time of sharing, that also could be arranged.

39

Difficult to Forgive

Q *Why do I find it so difficult to forgive someone who has deeply hurt me?* (*Martin*)

R As your accompanying letter makes plain, Martin, beneath your brief question is a deep well of grief and brokenness over fractured relationships in your life and family. It is easy for me, outside the immediate situation, to dispense what may be wholesome and wise counsel, for it is you who is undergoing hurt and suffering. I'm simply making it clear that what I am doing is listening, sharing some counsel that may help, and then, with you, laying the whole problem before our Lord. Let me apply some insights which others may also take up into their own lives where pain has been suffered in human relationships.

I am thinking now of some people who have come to me with such problems: the loving husband who discovered his wife was having an affair, and when it was ended he could not forgive her; the sister whose brother systematically took financial advantage of their mother up to and after her death, and who will not now speak to him; the daughter who is haunted by a sexual incident with her father in childhood, and years later cannot resolve the pain; the man whose fiancée abruptly broke off their engagement and who now feels rejected and unable to form a close relationship with another woman.

We can be so hurt, wounded and rejected by these affairs of the mind and heart that, after years of retreating into ourselves and not risking love again, we still have a wound which is deep, sore and unhealed. Or we feel violated and sinned against so that we cannot forgive, and thus find relief in tears, open sharing and reconciliation.

The analogies we use are significant: an open wound, a broken heart, a fragile psyche – images of vulnerability, weakness and suffering. Therefore the kind of person we need for help is not a judge but a physician – for we are sorely wounded and need the balm of sensitive sharing, the medicine of compassionate concern, the ointment of soothing tenderness. We need someone who will listen and understand, who will hold us and enter into our pain.

In my own experience I have found that tears often play an important part in the healing process. First of all there may be tears of anger or bitter regret at wounds afflicted upon oneself or by oneself upon others. In the context of listening, silence and receptivity, tears of confession appear, bringing the whole problem out of the dark place of retreat and into the healing light of sharing and love.

The whole process can fully be resolved if the two parties are together and there is a mutuality about this with mediated help; but even one person sharing his or her burden with a priest, pastor or soul friend can take the whole situation forward. Sometimes sharing is enough; sometimes it needs personal or sacramental confession; and sometimes it needs a bringing together of all concerned. It is here that tears of relief may be shed, with a mingling of sorrow and joy. This is but the beginning of a new chapter, for a relationship of gentle trust and increasing openness must be built upon that which had become fragmented and broken.

Sometimes a healing of memories is involved. It may be that there are unconfessed and unforgiven wrongs between children and parents, and one or more of the people have died. This is where sacramental confession and absolution can be of great help, or perhaps a requiem Eucharist where the whole matter is brought before the forgiving and healing Christ in the context of receiving communion. Michael Mitton and Russ Parker deal sensitively with this whole area in their book *Requiem Healing*.[1]

The healing of memories means that, with a good and sensitive pastor or soul friend, you can make the journey back into the area of breakdown, rejection or wounding so that healing tears can be shed, healing prayers said, and anointing and laying on of hands with words of for-giveness can be given. The place of despair then becomes the place of acknowledgement and letting go of resentments and obstinate attitudes, and God can bring us into a new relationship of forgiveness and recon-ciliation.

The reason why we find it difficult is because we have been wounded, our vulnerable souls have been grieved, our loving trust has been abused and rejected, and we are weak and human. But if we will simply take the first step and ask the Lord Jesus to accompany us, we can begin the journey that leads to restoration.

Reflection

However dark, deep and long is the problem, let us read through the above response prayerfully and begin the journey here and now. Seek out a trusted counsellor and friend and together start the process. The first step may be the most difficult, but perhaps you have already begun!

40

Controversy with Non-Believers

Q   *Is it wise to use polemics in discussion with a non-believer on the state of the world? (Iris)*

R   I'm all for discussion, debate and friendly controversy among all kinds of human beings, Iris, but 'polemic' is a powerful word – it means controversial or wordy warfare! I don't see any purpose in engaging in verbose wrangling or getting hot under the collar about religion or politics, though I do believe that there are times when a firm stand must be taken, albeit in a non-violent manner.

Such differences are not so often found between Christians and non-Christians, but between those who have a humanitarian attitude and lifestyle, and those who are materialistic and whose ideology is driven by money or power. In the political arena, a Christian may feel drawn to any of the major parties (I have difficulties with them all!). This is sometimes more of a temperamental bias, as Gilbert said in *Iolanthe*:

> Every boy and every gal
> That's born into the world alive
> Is either a little liberal
> Or else a little conservative

– though those lines are somewhat blurred these days! Yet such a trite jingle has some truth in it. We must try to get into the skin of those who argue with us on political or social issues – and the divide is likely to be found *within* the Church. As for arguing with non-believers on religious issues – well, by all means witness courteously, share insights and even indulge in gentle controversy – and if necessary disagree radically. But it is pointless to lose one's cool, score points, or even win an argument, for by brow-beating you can lose your opponent by winning the argument!

Sometimes it is necessary to decline to take issue because of the motivation and attitude of the opponent or the language of the debate. For instance, among the 'questions from a non-believer' that have come to me is one which begins: 'Christianity is a dogma that has possessed, polluted and perverted the human mind for two millennia'. I laid it aside because I'd like to see and know the person asking it, to sense their seriousness, and to discover whether such words are thrown in merely to wind me up!

Let me offer two pieces of counsel. First, be willing to get engaged with all kinds of people in questions religious, social and political, on as broad a spectrum as you can – for friendly dialogue can only serve to enrich experience and sharpen the mind.

Second, don't be afraid to disagree, while remaining friends or colleagues. If we parted company with all those who disagreed with us we would be very lonely! But in all of this remain honest, open, humorous. Integrity with a sense of humour is necessary in our world. We must be willing to lose arguments, but we must always be true to our conscience. So get at it!

Reflection

Let us look at our firmly-held views, and ask how far we are influenced by temperament, fears or conditioning, and how much we allow truth to challenge us. Perhaps the Holy Spirit is leading us to transformation!

41

Going Green

Q *I find it sad that the Church has little to say about green issues, and some Christians even think of it as worldly to get involved in such questions. Shouldn't the Christian Church be at the forefront of such questions?* (Steve)

R Well, it depends where you are coming from, Steve. Some groups of Christians, as you say, veer away from issues which involve an ecological perspective, animal rights or food quality fed to humans or animals. Some of them are concerned, they say, with the more important 'salvation of the soul' and see such issues as belonging to dubious New-Age groups. And yet these same people will support Trident, and the possession (and use) of a nuclear deterrent!

But things are changing, and even these groups are being shamed into awareness by the concerned non-Christians whose consciences are stirred by the cruelty to veal calves in their pens, battery hens in their cages, poisonous chemical fertilizers and a long list of ecological abuses and pollution.

It also has to be said that other parts of the Church are well into these issues, not only in their own communities but as members of the green movement generally.

Last week I had a visit from Susan, our local Green candidate, and though she is not a committed Christian, she affirmed that there was a clear interdependence between issues of spirituality and ecology. It was marvellous to share gospel issues with green issues, for they both have to do with the wholeness of our humanity – and that is salvation in a more profound sense. Jesus was concerned with the salvation (the basic word means health) of the whole person, and his compassion for the lonely, oppressed and sick was part of his ministry of forgiveness and reconciliation. It was all of a piece.

Susan brought with her a zealous member of Christian Ecology Link (CEL), and they were both enthusiastic about my green hermitage lifestyle! CEL's magazine is *Green Christians* (address at the back of this book), and it is a forum for events and issues in the wider green movement. It represents all Christian traditions, and the brief Basis of Faith runs:

> We affirm our belief in God as creator of all things and in Jesus Christ as Lord, looking to the Holy Spirit for guidance through the Scriptures, and seeking to hear him in the challenges of the present time.

This is not a green ghetto for Christians, for influence and sharing is encouraged, and Christians should be alert to these issues, whatever their political affiliation.

Of course, there is a price to pay for such responsibility. Abolishing battery systems for poultry, opposing long-distance transport of cattle for slaughter, the promotion of organic farming and setting right the massive abuses in these and other areas are costly. I constantly note that many Christians (especially clergy) are first to acquire expensive state-of-the-art computers, communication and media technology. There needs to be an immense shift in our priorities, or the world will laugh us to scorn.

I am also encouraged that our bishop of Worcester is well aware of green issues, and his new book *Grace and Mortgage* is allied to these concerns. Things are not as black as the question implies, but much greener!

Reflection

Let's look at our lifestyle. Is it based upon gospel values, or are we motivated by society's concern with acquisition, economic growth and consumerism? What changes need to be made? Will we make them?

42

Christians, Buddhists and Atheists Together

Q *Should not all like-minded people who strive for peace, justice and compassion in the world link together, whether they are Christians, Buddhists or atheistic humanists? Is not the real divide between those who will support any injustice for the sake of materialism and economic growth, and those who seek to live more simply so that a more equal sharing can take place? I realize that these are corporate as well as personal questions. (Russell)*

R It is not even as simple as that, Russell. There are religious, as well as atheistic materialists, who are so fixed in their ideological mind-set that they will persecute, maim and kill for the protection and spread of their ideology.

It is true that many millions of people were persecuted and massacred by the totalitarian regimes of Hitler and Stalin. But the religious history of the world is filled with hatred and bloodshed, and this applies especially to the three monotheistic religions.

This is a terrible backdrop to your question – the horrific picture of a fallen world in which the inhumanity of people towards each other is further exacerbated by our treatment of the animal world and of an increasingly threatened planet.

But there is another side to it, and this is where your question is relevant. Every sad story of contemporary conflict and bloodshed, earthquake or famine, is followed by compassionate financial and international team aid, and in our world there are many agencies of help for the alleviation of all kinds of suffering.

I believe that having the kind of militant and violent religion I've referred to is worse than having no religion. But in all the great world faiths there are men and women of peace and good will who seek only the common good of all races and peoples. Also, there are humanists who may be atheists or agnostics, but who are people of good will, and their objection to religion is often based on the problems we have referred to above. All such people of good will should (and do) band together in all kinds of agencies and efforts to bring peace, justice and aid to our beleaguered world. And yes, there is a very real divide between those who will support any injustice for the sake of ideology, materialism and economic profit, and those who desire peace, justice and equality. It is refreshing to read Hans Küng's *Global Responsibility: In Search of a New World Ethic.*[1] He looks not only for freedom, but for justice; not only equality, but also plurality; not only brotherhood but also sisterhood; not only coexistence, but peace; not only productivity, but solidarity with the environment; not only toleration, but ecumenism.

One of the reasons why I have given my life to the Franciscan vocation is because of the universalism of St Francis. He lived and acted towards all people, animals and creation in a brother–sister relationship, on the basis of a common humanity and creaturehood.

I have outlined this position in my book *Franciscan Spirituality,*[2] but of course it is not from Francis that this compassion originates, but from the Jesus of the gospels, whose love, light and healing should be channelled into the world through his Church.

But Christians cannot wait for a dynamic renewal of the *whole* Church, though they should strive for just that. They must continue to work for such renewal, and at the same time throw in their energies with any pacific group of people who are willing to be the instruments of good and light in our world.

Reflection

Am I part of the problem or part of the solution? Is my existence as an individual and as a relating person an instrument for greater light or darkness in the world? Without becoming depressed with evil, or obsessed with piety, does my lifestyle manifest a simple and warm humanity towards myself and others in the way of Jesus and St Francis? These questions, if shared with others, will lead to the right channelling of my contribution to the greater good, and this will reflect the ethics of the kingdom of God.

43

Changing Denominations

Q *Among my Christian friends I have a number who have changed denominations. I am a little confused about it because there are Roman Catholics who have become Anglicans, Anglicans who have become Roman Catholics, Baptists who have become Anglicans (and vice versa), and even a Pentecostal who has become Orthodox! Can it be true that they were guided by God, by truth or by temperament? Ought we not to try and stay where we are in these ecumenical days?* (Michael)

R Well, I'd better be frank, Michael, and confess that I am one of your culprits - from Baptist to Anglican in 1970 - but then you know that! I think of myself as an ecumenical Christian, and I would say first, that I was guided by the Spirit; secondly, that I treasured certain truths within the Anglican tradition; and thirdly, that there were strong temperamental factors involved in the change. But these do not wholly explain the move - it was all part of the pilgrimage in which I followed the leading of the Holy Spirit, and I retain a warm love and fellowship for my Baptist brothers and sisters.

Having said those things, I would add that there have been some who have passed me going in the opposite direction - and they also were guided. I left some truths behind when I moved (for example, baptism by immersion), and I acknowledge that there are devoted Christians who have different temperamental needs from mine in liturgy and worship.

But I also believe that some people change denominations unnecessarily, and for all kinds of negative reasons, finding themselves either still dissatisfied or with a convert mentality that becomes rigid and exclusivist.

If I had been Orthodox or Roman Catholic, I would not have moved - though I would have been unhappy about some aspects of these sister Churches and would have worked for positive change. But then I feel like that about the Anglican Church. Denominations have their benefits, as well as expressing the sad sin of division and disunity. There is only one Church, which is the Body of Christ, and all those who confess faith and love in the worship of God, Father, Son and Holy Spirit, are part of it, to whatever denomination they belong. They may be deficient or irregular in various doctrinal or sacramental ways, but then no one communion has all the truth.

You ask if we ought not to try to stay where we are in these ecumenical days. Well, generally I would say yes, but there are particular circumstances where this may not be possible or advisable. What we ought not to do is to cultivate or promote a convert mentality, or get involved in 'sheep-stealing'. I have Roman Catholic and Pentecostal friends who are equally devoted to Christ, and Anglican colleagues whose doctrine and practice do not match up to those of some of my Methodist friends! It is an amazing mixture, and there are good and bad Christians among charismatics, Catholics, Calvinists and monastics.

I think the best we can do in these days is to work together for a clearer experience and expression of the unity of the Church of God, and live in openness, love and peace with our fellow Christians. God calls us to proclaim and live the love and peace of Christ in our dark world, and if we do not do that, then sensible and wise non-Christians will have reason to deride us for our petty schismatic divisions and attitudes.

Reflection
We should each play our part in the many groups of ecumenical Christians, praying, learning, working and singing together for the praise of God and the good of all. Perhaps we could begin by sitting in Quaker silence, and attending a Roman Catholic Mass?

44

An Ecumenical Christian

Q *You often speak of yourself as 'an ecumenical Christian'. Can you be truly ecumenical and yet be faithful and loyal to your own communion and denomination? (Julia)*

R My straight answer is in the affirmative, Julia. This follows on from the last question about denominations (Chapter 43), but there are some blessings and warnings to be noted. First, the word 'ecumenical' is not popular in some quarters – it indicates to them compromise, reductionism in theology, a vague sentimentalism in respect of doctrinal truth and a lack of prophetic certainty.

My use of the word indicates none of these things, though I think the word 'compromise' is not such a nasty word – a bit more compromise in Northern Ireland would have saved lives and communities.

The word 'ecumenical' literally means living together in one household, and that is the household of Christian faith. I don't have to agree with all the beliefs and behaviour of my family in order to own them as relatives or to love them. Sometimes I love them in spite of themselves! I have a certain basic love and loyalty towards the Anglican Communion throughout the world, yet I still view it as the best of a bad lot among denominations! It is the Communion in which I find Catholic, Evangelical and ecumenical faith and practice to be alive and communicable. A high cost is paid for its comprehensiveness and breadth, but it enables me to affirm a strong Evangelical faith in the context of Catholic liturgy, church order and devotion, with intellectual and social concern which challenges and stretches me in all directions.

I acknowledge that there are Christians in other communions who treasure particular aspects of Evangelical, Catholic or intellectual truths more fervently in a different mix. But no one communion has a monopoly of truth. Basic Christian doctrines, worship, spirituality and lifestyles are shared across the denominational board and are not the prerogative of one denomination.

We are able in these days to share so much in all these and other areas, so that there is a warm ecumenical sharing and a greater sense of the unity of the one Body of Christ. Roman Catholic dissertations are being written on the positive value and witness of Martin Luther as a reformer and Karl Barth as a theologian. Baptists are serving as ecumenical officers in the World Council of Churches; the Methodist Sacramental Fellowship shares the eucharistic hymns of Charles Wesley, and John Wesley's universal vision and practice of sacramental confession; Anglicans are sharing theological training for ordinands with Orthodox, Roman Catholic and Free Church Christians. The charismatic movement is as likely to be found among Roman Catholics and Anglicans as among Pentecostals and house-church groups. Quaker writers are among the foremost teachers of spirituality, and the Salvation Army is willing to share and co-operate in united celebration among other Christians. URC, Brethren, Pentecostal and house-church Christians are likely to be found mingling with Catholic groups in retreat houses. The only communion which has not been represented in my small hermitage is the Lutheran – they are thin on the ground in this country, so the matter will soon be remedied!

Back to the question. I look forward to the day when denominations shall be no more, and the one Church of Christ will reflect the glory of God in truth and love. I do not believe that this will be an ecclesiastical union in one huge organization – that is not the unity envisaged in the New Testament. But I do long for a situation where there would be a mutual interchange of ministries, a mutual recognition of sacramental life, and a unity of heart in the love of Christ which rejoices in the one faith, and allows various strands and differences of interpretation and liturgy. The Anglican Communion has never seen itself in any exclusive sense, but only as *part* of the one, holy, catholic and apostolic Church, and perhaps it will have to disappear in the expression of a wider and deeper unity.

It may be that we shall not see such unity as I have just described before our Lord's second advent, but in the meantime we should be rehearsing such unity. And that I try to do, remembering Paul's words: 'Bearing with one another in love, making every effort to maintain the unity of the Spirit in the bond of peace' (Ephesians 4.2–3). Ecumenical is the word, and love and fervent enthusiasm is the practice, with heart and mind open to all that is joyfully human.

Reflection

Evaluate our own ecumenical attitude: is it wholesome, and reflected in our own church and group? How can we encourage ecumenical fellowship with other Christians in our area? As we answer these questions, we shall also share them with other Christians and expect the Lord to bless such endeavour.

45

A Doctor's Dilemma

Q *I am consulted by an increasing number of patients who want to postpone or deny death. I always desire to ease suffering, but the simple prolonging of life can become a macabre, clinical and loveless struggle against the inevitable. I believe in salvation for all who seek it in the heavenly after-life, but am I expected to be offering immortality in this one? (Andrew)*

R I believe you make a good and valid point here, Andrew, but it is precisely because you are a believing Christian physician that you can state it without fear. For it does seem to me that some in the medical profession are themselves either afraid of their own mortality, or they see a dying patient as an admission of failure.

I think of one of our Franciscan tertiaries who is also a GP, and who recently told me that he had encountered physical symptoms in himself that led him to believe that he may have to face terminal illness. And then he spoke of facing it with quiet acceptance, prayer and the decision to place the outcome in the hands of God. It turned out that the symptoms abated – but the experience gave him a new vantage-point in his own relationship with his patients.

In the materialistic, consumerist society in which we live it is clear why people think that they have the right to a happy, painless and pleasurable existence, for they are conditioned to believe that almost anything can be purchased at the right price. And it is important that they have it *now*, and that it continues indefinitely. So when they are faced with intractable physical limitations, degenerative disease or diagnosis of terminal illness, they expect by right or purchase to be freed from such catastrophe.

I do believe that there is no virtue in simply bearing pain, but that we should seek to alleviate it in ourselves and in others. But there comes a time when we must look our finitude and mortality in the face, and simply accept that we are going to die – and perhaps sooner than we thought.

I do not believe in easy access to euthanasia, but neither do I think it right or Christian to keep a person artificially alive in a vegetative state. There comes a time when people should be *allowed* to die but not *made* to die! In her book, *On Death and Dying*, Dr Elisabeth Kübler-Ross outlines five stages through which a person may go from first facing a terminal diagnosis to actually dying, based on her research with over 200 patients.[1] These five stages are:

- Denial;
- Anger;
- Bargaining;
- Depression;
- Acceptance.

It is well to get people thinking about such things for themselves and their loved ones before they happen – and perhaps part of our ministry is to help people do this. It would enable you to use your precious time more productively, rather than having to lead people through the terrible fear that they are going to die, when they have previously given no thought to the matter at all.

In this way you would not then be expected to prolong physical life for its own sake, but to help people enjoy this life in health or in sickness-limitation, with a gentle acceptance of the dying process when the time has come. This applies to your non-religious patients as well as your religious ones – those who have a healthy and mature faith should already have considered these matters, but sometimes Christians are notorious unbelievers!

Reflection

Why not spend a little time thinking prayerfully about St Paul's attitude to life and death in 2 Timothy 4.6–8, reading it in a quiet place? And then go for a meditation walk, considering your own health, mortality and eventual death in the light of the above response.

46

Is Euthanasia Always Wrong?

Q As a Christian I feel I ought to believe that euthanasia is morally wrong, but I think of some friends (mercifully not relatives) who have died painful, lingering deaths, with no real help in the alleviation of pain. I wonder whether I am more concerned about them rather than my own dying. I am not afraid of death itself, though I am apprehensive about the process of dying. So in the light of all this I wonder if euthanasia is always wrong? (Reg)

R This is a question which arises not only in our society generally, but among Christians too, and it raises a number of important points. The basic Christian principle is the sacredness of life. All life (especially human life) is to be treasured as a gift of God, and it is not our prerogative to take life – either another's or our own.

The word 'euthanasia' simply means 'a good death', and as Christians we should pray for a good and gentle death; but the term has come to mean, at best, the merciful ending of a person's life out of compassion. I say 'at best' because even if euthanasia were permissible and legal (as in some countries), it is open to medical or family abuse, and can raise difficulties if a person is mentally disturbed or depressed.

Are there, then, any occasions when a person may be helped to die, or enabled to take their own life? Basically my own feeling indicates a negative response – but there are occasions which make me think and pray over this matter again. I think of a woman doctor who took a fatal overdose after her diagnosis of terminal illness was confirmed. She knew well the suffering ahead, and left a note saying that she had no close relations who would grieve profoundly. She had decided rationally to end her life at that point, saving herself an unwanted and painful death, and saving the medical profession unnecessary and prolonged treatment.

I think also of a child with a brain tumour and secondary growths who could not bear to be touched because of the pain, and of a father who himself suffocated his child because he could no longer bear the sight and experience of the child's suffering.

Since the scourge of AIDS we hear of patients who decide to terminate their lives and get their friends to help them do so before the horrors of the disease overtake them.

These true stories halt me in my protestations and make me say, 'I understand', though I may not make of them the basis for the legalization of euthanasia. The hospice movement has done valiant work in the management of pain, making it possible for people to die without fear and surrounded by their loved ones at home or in hospice care. I wholly support the philosophy and work of the movement for which patients and families have reason to give thanks to God. But there remain some conditions in which dying can be a prolonged suffering for patients and their loved ones.

You see, I am not laying down a simple stern negative with no alternative. Rather I am stating a general binding principle of the sacredness of life, with warnings of abuse if euthanasia is legalized, but with the door open to exceptional circumstances and further thought.

As for the question – yes, I think it is right for us all to bring out our fears of death and dying, looking at them prayerfully and facing them honestly.

Reflection
Lay aside a period of time for meditation. Slowly read Psalm 23, and ask our Lord to help you think about your fears in the light of faith, and to strengthen your thinking and feelings in this matter, resulting in a trusting belief in his loving care as the One who will not forsake you in your hour of need.

47

Techniques without Love

Q *Of what use are techniques of prayer if we don't love God and one another? Shouldn't all our prayer be penitential? (Dominic)*

R The immediate answer to your question, Dominic, is that rituals without love are worse than useless, and that penitence is only a small part of the great adventure of prayer. But let me explain.

There is a classic passage in Micah's prophecy in which he castigates the mere ritual of bowing and scraping, burnt offerings, sacrifices and asceticisms, and asks what it is to come before the Lord. And the reply is:

> What does the LORD require of you
> but to do justice, and to love kindness,
> and to walk humbly with your God
> (Micah 6.8).

If you follow the great prophetic calls of the Bible, you will find that when God reveals himself in light, glory or vision, there is an immediate response of awe, wonder and penitence. But that is only the beginning. The call is followed by a specific revelation of the character and will of God, a declaration of his prophet's vocation, a commission for him to undertake, and the power and strength of the Lord's blessing, with the promise of his presence (see Exodus 3.1–17; Isaiah 6.1–8; Jeremiah 1.4–10).

Penitence and cleansing are basic in any prophetic call to holiness, but there follows a whole vocation of communion with God, and the communication of God's will to the people. So the life of prayer is the confrontation of the soul with the loving holiness of God. And though penitence leads to purification, that is only in order that the relationship of loving communion may take place. This must be an ever-deepening experience of the life of God in the soul, so that God's very character and image are reflected in the believer.

Because we have become entangled and enticed by sin, mesmerized by money, power and ambition, and sometimes dedicated to wickedness and the practice of corruption and evil, the process of sanctification may take a long time. After penitential confession and forgiveness, then by the grace of the Holy Spirit we may find that methods and techniques of stillness, prayer and communion are part of our journey, as well as sharing in the fellowship, liturgy and worship of the Church of God.

It goes without saying that the goal of all such preparation and discipline is that we may love God first, and that we allow that love to overflow to our neighbours and even to our enemies. This applies on a personal,

110

familial, corporate and even international level. There is here a whole lifetime's discipline in which prayer, penitence, discipline and love all run together in a whole life of dedication and devotion to the person of Christ, within the love of God.

So yes, the love of God is supreme, the love of neighbour is the consequence, and penitential prayer is a preparation for the whole of the mystical life which leads ultimately to participation in the Holy Trinity for all the children of God.

Reflection

Has my life of prayer moved from being sorry for my sins and asking favours for myself and my friends? Have I begun that adventure of prayer in which God is experienced in awe and wonder, and in which his image of love is reflected in my own life?

48

No Fire in my Belly

Q *I seem to be a half-hearted Christian. There is no fire in my belly. Where is suffering? Where is love? I do not truly love God.* (Philip)

R Fire in your belly, Philip? Well, I know of some wholly selfish fanatics who are wholehearted for their ideology, with plenty of fire in their belly, who take great pride in suffering, and in devotion to their cause will kill or maim.

If you look at the disciples you will find great temperamental differences. James and John, 'sons of thunder', could call down fire from heaven upon Christ's enemies; Peter was impetuous enough to cut off a soldier's ear in defence of his beloved master; Thomas was phlegmatic and cautious, but was faithful enough to want to go to Jerusalem and die for Jesus.

It is not those who make great claims, shout loud affirmations and stir up fiery enthusiasm who are necessarily the most committed Christians.

Perhaps you envy those up-front people whose temperament is different from your own, who seem to be wholehearted because they are sanguine and hearty, who have more of the gift of loquacity than of sympathy, but you are not to know that.

Of course, you may be right. You may be half-hearted, cold, evading suffering because you do not truly love God. But if that is so, then it sounds as if you are painfully aware of it, and that very feeling may be born of the Holy Spirit. I think you should follow these feelings through in prayer, and God will lead you on.

Recognize that there are red-hot mystics, like the Spaniard St John of the Cross, or the Italian Jacopone da Todi – or St Francis himself. But there are also gentle English mystics, like Lady Julian of Norwich and the unknown author of *The Cloud of Unknowing*, and there are philosophical mystics like Meister Eckhart and those of the Rhineland school.

Dedication to Christ is of the mind, the heart and the body, and devotion to Christ may be manifested in the basic dynamic which drives you on in vision and creativity. Therefore your Christian calling could be as a contemplative in a cloister, a prisoner of conscience in a cell, a scientist in a laboratory, a doctor or nurse serving lepers or AIDS patients, a martyr in a totalitarian political regime – I could go on!

You see what I am saying? Fire in the belly means different things to different people, and a knowledge of ourselves, of who we are and what we are capable of, is basic to the enterprise. I did not mention musicians in the last paragraph, but suppose Mozart, Bach or Beethoven had been denied access to music and had been forcibly put to law, medicine or politics. Not only would there have been no fire in their belly, but there would have been such frustration that may have led them to despair, for they would not have been fulfilling that for which they were born.

So how does one know? We are not all geniuses like Moses, Mozart or Einstein, but in our own small way we must get to know ourselves. That means prayer, self-evaluation, a priest or psychiatrist, or perhaps a retreat using the Myers-Briggs Type Indicator or the Sufi Enneagram course. Even as I write these words, I hear an inward voice saying: 'You know these are only later helps along the way – who and what you are is much more basic and reaches into childhood and the awareness of the roots of your being'. That voice indicates my own experience, for my childhood awareness and dreams were not negated by others or repressed by myself, and I know that many people grow out of and away from their childhood and have to begin again later in life. Perhaps I am saying that you may have been frustrated at some point in your early life, and that you took a wrong turn somewhere along the way, and your feeling of 'no fire in your belly' is a cry of frustration; you may have to retrace your steps, by the grace of God – and for that you will need help.

We all reflect the image of God in different ways, and the fire begins to burn when our feet are on the right path. We must not ape others but find our own way. By a deeper knowledge of ourselves, we will come to a deeper knowledge of God, for he will be with us in all our searching. If we have to retrace our steps and go back to that place or decade where we began to deny 'the real me', it will not be a waste of time or energy, for there is a beautiful Scripture which says: 'I will repay you for the years that the swarming locust has eaten' (Joel 2.23). There is a hidden and secret flame which has been covered by the debris of the years, perhaps. If this is so, and we begin to clear away the rubbish, it will begin to burn again, and frustration will give way to fulfilment.

Reflection
If you feel that this chapter's question may apply to you, read through Charles Wesley's hymn, 'O Thou who camest from above', and share it and this chapter with a trusted friend, beginning an open discussion about your life and pilgrimage.

49

Stick-and-Carrot Theology

Q *I do believe in the Christian hope of eternal life, but I don't like the stick-and-carrot idea of reward and punishment after death. If I found that there was no life after death, it would not affect the life I live now, for I do not want my present life to be conditioned by the threats or promises of the life to come. Does this make sense?* (Peter)

R Make sense, Peter? Well yes, and no. I mean that if there is a moral law which is for the common good, we should all want to live by it. But we need not object to penalties for rupturing that good, or to consequential blessings following the keeping of it, though we should not behave to escape penalties or obtain blessings.

But I do understand what you are saying. To follow the life, love and teaching of Christ is fullness of joy in itself, and ought not to be an insurance policy against penalties or assurance policy for credits. I think the Quaker, John Whittier, got it right:

> Alone, O Love ineffable,
>   Thy saving name is given;
> To turn aside from thee is hell,
>   To walk with thee is heaven.[1]

If I was told today that there was no life beyond, and that all the 'eternal life and death' language of the Bible was to be interpreted into this life alone, I would continue to love and follow Christ, for that is an inward imperative for me – but, I must admit, my hope and anticipation would be greatly diminished.

It is not possible to drive a wedge between who and what Jesus was in his earthly ministry and the continuance of his relationship with his people through and beyond death. It simply means that when we choose Christ, we choose love and healing, hope and joy – now and forever! And if we reject Christ and choose darkness, evil and egocentricity, then we actually place our feet on the path of lostness that leads, by nature of the choice, to death. You cannot break the package open and be choosy!

The mystical tradition is clear about this: you look at the radiant love crucified on the cross and you weep in penitence and adoration; you gaze upon the unutterable beauty of God and you fall in love. There is no penalty or reward, for the question and the answer is love. This simple translation of a piece from St John of the Cross brings me to tears:

> I am not moved, my God, to love you
> By the heaven you have promised me.
> Neither does hell, so feared, move me
> To keep from offending you.
>
> You move me, Lord, I am moved seeing you
> Scoffed at and nailed on a Cross.

I am moved seeing your body so wounded
Your injuries and your death move me.

It is your love that moves me, and in such a way
That even though there were no heaven, I would love you,
And even though there were no hell, I would fear you.

You do not have to give me anything so that I love you,
For even if I didn't hope for what I hope,
As I love you now, so would I love you.[2]

Reflection

The divine love completely reorientates our thinking. We understand
that compassion and beauty spring forth from the divine fecundity, and
that is the source, centre and end of the grace that draws us to God.

50

Ethical Church Commissioners?

Q *How can the Church expect Christians to live exemplary lives when the
Church Commissioners, in their leaflet on ethics, unambiguously state that
making money is their top priority, and if ethical concerns tally with this, all
the better. They also consider it to be ethical to invest in companies that spend
up to 25 per cent of budget on the arms trade. Is this but one example of dou-
ble standards, which accounts for a general dissatisfaction regarding institutional non-ethical behaviour?* (Paul and Louise)

R I looked at your question, Paul and Louise, and was stirred up by the
kind of attitude that prompted it. I thought, 'Here are two firebrands,
and I'm with them in their concerns'. But I know how easy it is to be
so fired with enthusiasm for a vital ethical (or doctrinal) matter that
one's quotations and presentation become more emotional than factual!

So I got hold of the current Church Commissioners' material to check out the facts, and though I did not find a direct reference to the matter of '25 per cent of budget on the arms trade', I was nevertheless more disturbed by their material than by your question!

Let me try to respond with some understanding. The Church Commissioners have a task, a 'commission' to produce a proper return on their assets for the support of parochial ministry. One would therefore expect that this laudable task would have the kind of priorities which do not allow responsible secular agencies to discern ethical ambiguities in investments.

So when the literature says that financial considerations must be uppermost in investment decisions, I would hope that this does not mean that ethical compromise is involved for better financial return. There is an Ethical Investment Policy which operates, and in 1994 a Church Ethical Working Group was established which brings together the Church's main central investing bodies. This provides a focus for the examination and discussion of ethical issues – and with the growth of large conglomerates this task is increasingly complex, so the job is not an easy one.

Account is taken of the strongly held views of members of the Church – and that means that there is no investment in companies whose main business is armaments, gambling, alcohol or tobacco. But I don't like the sound of that 'whose *main* business'. GEC, for example, has a focused interest in 'defence', particularly electronic-related equipment. A problem arises when you distinguish between offensive and defensive equipment, and when some products have both civil and military uses.

I must be open about my own pacifist stance, and therefore I am not impressed by the argument that there are some 86,000 employees in GEC, and that the products are used by our armed forces to defend the nation. We've heard these kinds of arguments before, and elsewhere!

The moral issues are complex, and the Church Commissioners' literature gives me the impression that there is a genuine desire for ethical investment – but they are an ecclesiastical institution which, like the Vatican Bank and its subsidiaries, needs to be watched, monitored, with regular checks and informed debate and protest in public.

The Church Commissioners continue to provide needed financial support for the Church's ministry, and we must be fair and appreciative of their work. In 1995 they sold their shares in BSkyB because of the decision to broadcast the Playboy Channel, so disinvestment is possible. The present ban on breweries and distilleries is under review, and the reason given is the changing of social attitudes towards alcohol consumption and the industry's shift of emphasis towards family leisure provision. I don't like the sound of that!

If ethical issues are compromised, then I believe the price is too high. In such cases I believe we should disinvest, and if that means financial loss (which it does), then we must reduce, simplify and radically economize. We must support and pray positively for the whole work of the Church of God, and be open to fair-minded secular people in their questioning of our beliefs and actions in the market-place.

Reflection

Why not get hold of the up-dated literature on ethical investments from the Church Commissioners Information Office (address at the back of this book). Examine it, debate it with Christian and non-Christian friends, and through the General Synod make your views known with appropriate action. Such action may be positive and appreciative of the Church Commissioners, and it may be constructively critical – but let it always reflect integrity with humility.

PART FOUR

Questions from Non-Believers

51

Churchgoers Put Me Off!

Q *Christians talk about good news of freedom, and new life through Christ. Why then do I feel so unimpressed with many who call themselves Christians? I'd like to be a Christian, but many churchgoers put me off. What do you think? (Gareth)*

R When I was a curate in Glasgow, one day a tramp outside the church tried to sell me a pair of brown boots. As we talked, he said: 'Are you a priest in that church there?' I said I was, and his comment was salutary: 'They're a load of hypocrites!' I replied: 'Well yes, but we're trying to do something about it!'

He went off, and the following Sunday morning from the pulpit I told the congregation what he had said. They chuckled because I told them with a grin on my face, but then I asked them how serious a comment it was, and what they and I were going to do about it.

It's a problem – for though I think the man was a bit jaundiced about St Mary's congregation (they were a great crowd), I also wonder if anyone, in the name of Christ, had ever loved him, opened their hearts and their purses to him, or given him the warmth and compassion that Christ would have shown.

There was a great gulf fixed between the congregation (which had a good proportion of poor people and students), and this man of the road, and though his objection was not the same as yours, Gareth, it was even more damning.

I do openly and freely acknowledge that this country is full of Christian churches and institutions which are part of the establishment scene. Many of them, of all denominations, are doing a good and solid work in many areas – but they also contain many people who are what

I call 'professing but not possessing'. By that I mean that the vital and dynamic gospel life has not taken hold of them and transformed their lives, empowering them to show the love, joy and peace which was so evident in the faith and practice of the early Church.

But I must also say that there are many Christians, again in all denominations, who are filled with Christ's love and from whom his radiance shines. After all, you say that you would like to be a Christian, so you must have seen some manifestation of the Christ-life.

I could call upon many witnesses in the early and recent history of the Church to prove the power and genuineness of the gospel. I could also talk about friends whose lives have undergone thorough conversion, and who are on the way to becoming the kind of Christians that you expect to see. But let me pitch it at a personal level.

I came from a loving, but not specifically religious home, yet was influenced by the witness of the Church from an early age. When I was 12, I had a definite meeting with Jesus Christ at a missionary service in which a team of young men and women, who were just off on their first assignment abroad, shared their witness of how Christ had met them, called and equipped them to love and serve him overseas. The zeal and joy of this team, and especially of one young woman, caught my attention, and I longed to know the same quality of enthusiasm that so deeply moved me. So that evening I surrendered my young life to Christ, and from that moment to this very day he has been real and precious to me. Everything I have ever learned and done in my life which has been good and true is because of Christ. I owe my life and joy, my education and enthusiasm, my communicative abilities and love of people to him. And if I am among the redeemed people of God, it is because he loved me, and gave himself to win me to his fold.

As I write now, my heart overflows with simple joy because I can look back over the joys and sorrows of my life and say that Christ has been with me every step of the journey, sometimes leading me in obedience and trust, and sometimes having to rescue me from the wrong path, the Slough of Despond or from Vanity Fair!

I am conscious that Christ will never leave me, whatever lies in the future, and he will bring me at last to his kingdom of joy and peace. In all this, the ministry of the Church has been fundamental, and though I owe the greatest debt to the Anglican and Baptist Communions, I find increasing fellowship with all kind of Christians from across the confessional boundaries, and look forward to that day when the Church will experience the fullness of its unity in the Holy Spirit.

I have talked about my personal experiences because it grieves me to think that you are turned away by whatever deficiencies you have found among some Christians. May I ask that you will nevertheless look to the Christ who calls you to himself. If you already desire to be one of his disciples, he yearns to receive you more than you desire to follow him. Look again at the gospels, open your heart in simplicity to Christ's call, and ask him to receive you and fill you with his Spirit.

Reflection

Here are two suggestions.

- Find an open church and take with you this Scripture which you have written out: Jesus said:

  'Come to me, all you that are weary and are carrying heavy burdens, and I will give you rest. Take my yoke upon you, and learn from me; for I am gentle and humble in heart, and you will find rest for your souls. For my yoke is easy, and my burden is light.' (Matthew 11.28-30)

  Kneel or sit in quiet gratitude that Christ will do his part and open up your being that he may fill you with his Spirit.
- Send for daily Bible reading material in the quarterly booklets of the Bible Reading Fellowship or Scripture Union (addresses at the back of this book), and you will soon find your roots going down into the sustaining love of God which already holds you in life – then look at the Church again!

52

Christianity Makes People Worse!

Q *To me, Christianity seems to change people for the worse. How can I put my faith in something which breeds such narrow-minded, prejudiced and judge-mental people? (Richard)*

R You come on fairly strong, Richard – but I have to admit that I have also found people who are not improved by their 'taking on religion'. You will notice, throughout this book, that I make a distinction between religion – even Christianity – and the Christ. A good canon of genuine-ness is this: 'Does my religion make me a more human, loving, com-passionate person, or less?' If the answer is less, then chuck it!

There is great power in religion, but it can be a power for ill. It can twist and pervert judgement, it can oppress, threaten, torture and kill. When politicians have sought to harness that power, it usually turns out for evil. But it can also inspire the greatest art, music, architecture, science and medical research.

If I were not a Christian, I would really be puzzled that while there exist good, peaceable, loving Hindus, Buddhists, Muslims, Jews and Christians, there are also within those faiths men and women (usually men!) who are hungry for power, ambition and money. These people are so ideologically blinkered that they become exclusivist and think that they have a monopoly on truth and that all other views must be muz-zled or persecuted. When they are in a minority they are like a lamb, when in equality like a fox, and when in majority like a wolf!

Does all this sound strange coming from a Christian? My response is far more fierce than this provocative question. And why, then, do I gladly count myself among those who are religious? Well, it is better *not* to be religious if it is that negative, persecuting and exclusivist kind of religiosity. But I am a follower of the one whose life was full of sympathetic healing and forgiveness; who spread light and truth, and even in his death loved and forgave his persecutors, encouraging his followers to do the same.

124

Well, what has happened since then? The Christian faith, in the fourth century, became increasingly patronized by the state, then accepted and established. That was the beginning of popular corruption, as always happens when politics and religion make an agreement based on material power, wealth and authority. We are still struggling with this, so that on a personal level one kind of corruption is evident, and on a national level another kind. You have been the unfortunate witness to either a sect-like religion that exclusivizes and excludes, or to the kind that has led to hypocrisy and material corruption. The televangelists' financial and moral corruption represents one kind, and state–religious persecution (as in Bosnia, and elsewhere) another.

I would encourage you not to take on board such religion, but to challenge it wherever you find it. At the same time, do not yourself become negative and judgemental in a secular kind of bigotry, but look at Christ's life and determine that compassion will be the measure of your judgement and the pattern of your life. Then I shall greet you as a brother.

Reflection
We must try to differentiate between those who are merely religious, and those who truly live in the love of Christ. And we should seek to learn and practise universal sympathy in our own lives.

53

Seeking Faith – Unfriendly Church

Q *I am a widower, and have worked hard all my life, with my share of knocks and disappointments. Now in my old age I don't feel that God is close to me, and I have found the Church unfriendly and unhelpful. I would like a living faith, but what can I do? (Bill)*

R It is clear, Bill, that you have not been on the receiving end of much help, and the first thing you need is someone to whom you can relate in trust, with the support of a welcoming and hospitable group of people – which the Church is meant to be! I can well believe what you say about the unfriendliness of your local church, but it is not always like that, and I'd advise you to try again – in another church.

But I also want you to consider that you may be wrong in one thing – when you say, 'I don't feel that God is close to me'. Your feelings may be simply reflecting your difficult experiences, and the reality may be much more positive. I would suggest that whatever your emotions are telling you, God is for you, and closer to you than you can imagine. If you said that you felt that *you* were not close to God, that may be nearer the truth – though again, you may be closer than you think.

Nevertheless, you have to begin where you are, and the fact that you are desiring a living faith means that your face is towards God, and therefore he desires to send his ray of love into just that chink of openness that invites him. Perhaps you might think about spending a few days at one of our Franciscan guest-house friaries or convents. There you will not only be able to share in some of the life with guests, sisters and brothers, but you will find that lively and warm fellowship that you have not so far discovered in the Church.

As I think of you linked up with a friary visit, I see you going on to try again in a local church with the friary experience behind you. Perhaps a different church may delight you with its welcome. Then you will be able to ask about transport to services if needed, or house communion and sick visits if and when necessary.

If you are able to get about, then you may even find a house-group meeting which will reflect some of your interests, for many churches are into all kinds of new areas these days. So you may suddenly find that you are a square peg in a square hole!

Reflection

Have I thought that God may have a role and a task for which he needs *me*? It may be that I can link together people like myself who need a hand of friendship, and I could then become a link-person between them and a friendly church.

54

Conditioned to be a Christian

Q My atheist friends say that I am only a Christian because I was brought up as one. Does this devalue my belief? (Trevor)

R I wonder, Trevor, if some of your atheist friends may themselves be the subject of their own social conditioning? I cannot help but think that being confronted by such a possibility yourself can only be good, for it will help you to sort out your conditioning, upbringing, temperamental needs and objectivity in regard to your faith. Of course, it may well be that you are, in many ways, who and what you are because of parental pressure, social conditioning and cultural mores. But we do live in a multifaceted society in which we are challenged on every side, and unless we live in a religious ghetto, we shall respond to both accusation and encouragement with a certain lively openness that keeps us on our toes.

I am sure that many of us are professing Christians because we have been subjected to parental, educational, societal and personal influences which have brought us to where we are. But some of us have reacted against such influences, and in my own case a loving, but non-dogmatic home, an unbelieving peer group at school and a few really antagonistic teachers helped to confirm my Christian stance. Yet all of that was secondary. The main influences upon me were my natural sense of wonder as a child and the exposure to the mystery of creation.

I had a Celtic inheritance in terms of the created order, and though it was not at first specifically 'God', but 'wonder and mystery', I soon related the two together in my later Christian teaching. Also, in contrast to the antagonistic teachers, there were two or three who were so filled with warmth and joy, and with affection for us boys, that I identified myself with their quiet faith. I think of Noel Davies saying, 'Now boys, remember, those who take the sword shall perish by the sword', when I was ten years of age – and I realize that this not only encouraged my natural pacifism, but it also made me aware that there were others who felt the same way.

Antagonism and confrontation in the school yard actually encouraged me to stand firm for the values of Christ, and I found myself not only able to stand against the cynicism and bullying of my peer group, but avidly willing to engage in debate and disagreement. And this has stood me in good stead.

None of this challenging examination of ourselves devalues the faith of those who have been born, brought up and influenced powerfully towards Christian confession, as long as those people are open enough to listen, examine and test their faith, and are willing to change if persuaded by the truth.

I also believe that all those who have been brought up in other faiths and traditions, if they are sincere in their belief, open and honest in their lives, and have their faces towards love and truth – then whatever their religious background and conditioning, their life and stance has spiritual value, which cannot be devalued or trashed by cynicism or unbelief.

Reflection

Reflect upon your own childhood, community and upbringing, giving thanks for all the positive influences; and be prepared to strive for integrity and honesty in your beliefs and behaviour as a responsible human being.

55

Britain a Christian Country?

Q *Is Britain still a Christian country? (Ian)*

R The big assumption in your brief question, Ian, is that Britain ever was a Christian country – indeed, that there could ever be such a thing! Certainly it is difficult to think of countries as Christian in these days of increasing secularism, and with the multicultural face of our society.

So let's ask three questions:

- Was Britain ever Christian?
- Has secular materialism swept away even the semblance of Christian life and witness?
- Does a multicultural secular society threaten Christian values?

First, to claim to be a Christian country involves ambiguity, for there are no specifically 'Christian' states. From a New Testament standpoint the Church was meant to bear witness in and among all nations as a leavening influence, being salt and light, living and preaching gospel values in imperfect societies. Christian citizenship is primarily a heavenly one (Philippians 3.20), though this should make Christians better citizens on earth. When there was a conflict of interests in the early Church, then the will of God was primary, and this held from the time when the state was considered to be a power for good (Romans 13.1–7), into the period when the persecuting emperors were considered to be Antichrist (throughout the book of Revelation).

The big change took place when the Emperor Constantine claimed to have had a visionary conversion to Christianity in 313. He evolved a politico-religious regime in which the cross became the sign of temporal power, and the Church found itself lured by establishment values.

As Thomas Merton points out in *The Wisdom of the Desert*,[1] the Desert Fathers, who retreated into the desert in reaction to the pagan takeover, doubted that there could be such a thing as a Christian state, or that Christianity and politics could ever mix to such an extent as to produce a fully Christian society.

Merton counters the accusation that these scandalous views simply meant a negative withdrawal, with no effective way of meeting the problems of the age. It was precisely these desert people who did meet contemporary problems, for they were ahead of their time, and they opened the way for the development of a new society. Regression to a herd mentality was their fourth-century problem, and it is the inspiration of such desert saints of principle and dynamic that gives access to a vital spiritual life which leads to the social and common good.

This desert community would not be ruled by a decadent state, nor be passively moulded by the morals, values and policies of a temporal power impregnated by ambition, authority and violence. They were eminently social in a gospel mode, but their authority was the charismatic wisdom and experience of love, not of manipulative politics.

There has been a tremendous surge of interest in these Desert Fathers and Mothers and in their hermit and community tradition, for they carry on the New Testament witness of being 'in the world and yet not of the world' (John 17.14–19), influencing the state for good, but witnessing against all forms of inhumanity and oppression.

When we ask questions about our own country's status as Christian, it is well to look back to this watershed of Christian witness where the persecuted Church became the established Church.

At this point let us look at the second question of whether secular materialism has swept away vital Christian witness. There is no doubt that our society and our religious integrity has been damaged by materialistic values which deny any spiritual dimension to human life. A society which lays aside spiritual values loses a sense of the sacredness of life. In the atheistic Marxism which has now collapsed in the former Soviet Union a great deal of inhumanity and oppression was evident, but the capitalist consumerist ideology which is taking its place may well itself be devoid of the spiritual life which survived underground under the old regime. As we begin a new millennium it is well for us to hear words spoken by Alexander Solzhenitsyn in 1993:

> Although the earthly ideal of Socialism–Communism has collapsed, the problems it purposed to solve remain: the brazen use of social advantage and the inordinate power of money, which often direct the very course of events. And if the global lesson of the twentieth century does not serve as a healing inoculation, then the vast red whirlwind may repeat itself in entirety.[2]

Yet there are encouraging signs among humanitarian non-religious people, and a great yearning for spiritual values in many places in our society, and I believe that the Christian Church and other religious traditions must struggle to maintain their witness. In struggle, vitality is renewed and dedication sharpened, and this augurs well for the future.

This brings us on to the matter of a multicultural society. The Christian faith has been the majority religion in Britain for centuries, and we have been thought of as a Christian nation, though the values of the old empire were hardly covered by this religious cloak.

The Reformation shook up the whole matter in a unique manner in Britain, and though the state rightly cast off the pope's political interference, the Church was saddled with a monarch as its supreme governor.

There is an interesting contemporary debate on the disestablishment of the Church of England. I find myself in the novel situation of having been confirmed in the disestablished Church in Wales, ordained as priest in the Episcopal Church in Scotland and ministering in the established Church of England! The Anglican Communion is a strange animal, and it must be remembered that the Church of England is the only established Church throughout the worldwide Anglican Communion.

I also find it interesting when I hear people of other faiths affirm that they would prefer the Church of England to continue as the established Church, for they feel more secure with a communion which would handle the multi-faith order fairly and with integrity. Perhaps there is enough here to keep you thinking, especially if you recall that a future monarch, along with many other changes, may take the title 'Defender of Faiths'! But that is another question.

Reflection
Let us keep abreast of informed debate in areas of radical Christian witness in the midst of a secular society, and work towards linking with all people of spiritual values as leaven in our social mixture.

56

The Problem of Suffering

Q *I don't want to call myself an atheist, but I can't really believe in God because the world doesn't make sense. Quite apart from the world's suffering which I've only heard and read about, I am faced with people I've known who have suffered terminal illnesses, and especially the pain and deaths of innocent children. How can there be a God of love when all this is allowed? (Joe)*

R Your question, Joe, is one which has come to me over and over again in its different forms. It is the perennial question we call the 'problem of suffering'. It can be stated like this: 'If God is loving and he does not stop such suffering, he cannot be all-powerful; if he is all-powerful and does not stop it, he cannot be loving.'

This kind of questioner thinks of God as an almighty power-figure, sitting in the heavens, who does or does not grant prayers or sends and withholds judgement. I am going to give you a reverent 'I don't know' at the end of this response, for it is not quite as simple as the way I've reframed your question: there is no big, mighty God sitting 'somewhere' who is either unloving or causing confusion. 'God' is the name we have for the life-giving dynamic Spirit which flows throughout creation, imparting meaning, beauty and compassion wherever there are those who are open to those creative impulses and powers.

I hitched a lift from a lorry driver before I came to my hermitage, and he put this question to me as we were travelling on the A303. He started off by saying he was an atheist, and in framing his question he said that he had known a family who died in a tragic house fire, and this personal element had confronted him with the problem.

I listened and sympathized and told him that I well understood and didn't blame him at all for the way he felt, for it was my problem too. But I had another problem, for his evidence wasn't the only evidence that presented itself. I called my other problem the 'problem of beauty'. He looked puzzled and asked what I meant. I told him that, as he related his sad reasons for not believing in a God of love, I was thinking of the glad reasons for being drawn to such a belief.

In the world as I experience it, as well as the obvious pain and sorrow which we know well enough, there is also a design and harmony, a balance and a beauty found around us and within. It is found in the rhythmic cycle of the seasons, the melody of music, art and poetry, and especially in the many expressions of love between human beings. There is delight in the laughter and playfulness of little children, the joy of parents, the ecstasy of lovers, the affection of friendship and the solid faithfulness of older people. All these, together with all the creative and joyful impulses in our world, are celebrated on a popular level by Louis Armstrong singing 'It's a Wonderful World'.

All this I told the lorry driver, adding that my immense enthusiasm for life, from childhood to the present day, has filled me with the affirmation of the God who comes in joy and sorrow to meet me. I said: 'You pays your money and you takes your choice, and if it is a gamble, then I gamble my life on God and on love'.

'I've never thought of it like that before', he said. And then I went on to tell him about the special evidence of the man Jesus Christ – I've laid that out in the next chapter in this book. Then I said that it seemed to me that, in order to make some positive sense of life, choosing the 'God path' allowed my life to be lived for the greatest good of all, including myself.

He then turned his head while driving and said: 'If I wasn't an atheist, what could I be without fully believing in God?' 'Well', I replied, 'you could take the position, just for the present, as an agnostic – one who simply does not know.' 'Right', he grinned. 'I think I'll be an agnostic.' The conversation ended there – but I don't believe his thinking did.

There is other evidence, for I am no agnostic – I really do believe. Not because I have discovered 'It', but rather because 'It' has found me. But read on to the next chapter, and I hope you will find that the same gentle influence is at work in your life.

Reflection

Why not try a simple experiment. Write the following prayer on a card, and for the next month, at the beginning of each day, suspend your unbelief, take a risk, and say the words, and be aware during the days of 'something' that may cause you to think again:

O God, if there be any God, send your Spirit to open my eyes and heart to the truth whatever it may be, and wherever it may be found. Amen.

I hope you may be surprised at the outcome!

57

Inequalities, Injustice, Imbalance

Q   *Patients ask me frequently, as their doctor, why God allows such suffering and why 'good people' die young. What are your thoughts on these questions?* (Antony)

R   You are a Christian doctor, Antony, and I know that you consciously ally yourself with the healing power of God in our world, and see your role in the alleviation of pain and suffering.

My response to the previous question (Chapter 56) spoke of the problem of suffering with which your questions are concerned, but also with the design, pattern, cyclic rhythm and meaning – which I called the 'problem of beauty' in our haphazard world.

But let me make the point of haphazardness. There is something obviously wrong in our world, and to a believer who affirms basic purpose, meaning, joy and even love at the heart of all things, this constitutes a real problem. That is why theologians speak of 'original sin'. This is a misnomer, for there is nothing original about sin! Indeed, it is misleading – for sin, brokenness, disintegration, imbalance, disharmony and things 'out of kilter' were not God's desire for his world, and are not now. If anything is original, it is life, light, joy and hope – summed up in the word love. In spite of all, I believe that love is at the heart of all things, but it is not possible for us to demonstrate this beyond doubt, because first, the world is out of harmony with its maker, and secondly, human beings are themselves alienated morally, so there is an ambivalence within us, and within the world in which we live.

Am I saying, then, that there is a way to see things more clearly, and to find a path which leads to an experiential understanding of all this, together with the possibility of linking with and spreading such love?

Well yes, I am. If taken, this path or discipline will not do away with the objective suffering of our world, nor will it stop 'good people' dying young. But it will do two things. First, it will enable seekers to understand, at least in part, why things are as they are. And this will produce a consequent change of attitude which can turn their hurts into healing – along the pattern of the wounded healer. Then it will give them the insight, direction and energy to become part of the loving agency in the world (which is the Holy Spirit), leading people towards the healing of the world's ills. Those who are wounded become the healers because they understand what it is to bear the pain of suffering, loneliness, rejection and humiliation. This is simply to follow the pattern of the Christ who was despised and rejected, who went down into death, but rose by the power of God – the wounded healer who heals the fallen world.

Of course, it is not possible simply to pattern our lives upon Christ's by an act of the will, especially if we ourselves are cast down into the pit of suffering and helplessness. We cannot extricate ourselves from the pit by wanting to, or by moral or intellectual effort. That is why we must look to Christ first of all as Saviour. He comes to where we are, bringing with him his forgiving love, his healing power. As we confess our utter need to him in penitence and faith, that is the place where the healing begins. It is at that point that he grants us the indwelling of his Holy Spirit, and it is this Spirit who reproduces in us the pattern of the wounded healer, and we become simply channels of *his* help and healing to others.

Moving back to the questions – there is a certain mystery about sin, sickness and inhumanity which we cannot understand in our present state of knowledge. Although God 'allows' them (and that is bound up with human freedom), he does not desire them. The father of the prodigal son allowed his son to claim his inheritance, go off into a far country and there dissipate his money in immoral and riotous living. This led the son into frustration, famine and near starvation, which was not his father's will or choice. When the son was at the end of himself, starving and penitent, he was ready to make his way back. Even when he was a long way off, the father was watching for him, ran towards him, embraced him in complete forgiveness, and called for joy and celebration at his return (Luke 15.11–32).

Some of the pain of this mystery is told out in the tragic experience of the son of Rabbi Harold Kushner, and his experience addresses the second part of our question.[1]

The infant was diagnosed with progeria, or rapid ageing, and in his book, *When Bad Things Happen to Good People*, Rabbi Kushner relates the harrowing story, leading to the death of the boy at 14 years old.

Rabbi Kushner emerges as a more mature man and pastor, but with a courageous honesty and sadness in which he shares the pain and darkness of our world, and in the process he himself becomes a light in a dark place.

I have encountered physical, mental and spiritual affliction and pain in the most sensitive and creative people, and the amazing thing is that it has transformed many of them into such perceptive and spiritual persons who are able to reach out to others in healing precisely because they have known such suffering themselves. I am *not* preaching that suffering is ennobling – it is frequently devastatingly destructive. Nor am I saying that God sends such suffering – that is almost blasphemous! But I am saying that, given that such suffering exists, I have constantly been amazed at the way in which the actual sufferers have turned it to good, to healing and even to love.

Reflection

Let us consider prayerfully the way in which the pattern of Christ can be reproduced in our own lives, not by our ascetic efforts, but by the interior indwelling of the Holy Spirit. This means the surrender of ourselves to allow the life of Christ to radiate from us – and this involves a deeper life of prayer. This is a costly prescription for any Christian, but the prognosis is abundant life.

58

Christian or Secular Funeral?

Q *I don't really believe in God and therefore I think it would be hypocritical for me to have a Christian funeral. I'm not sure what I am asking – perhaps I want to know if it's right for me to make such a decision for myself, knowing my relatives may be hurt or embarrassed, though others may approve of such a decision. Also, what would you, as a Christian, say are the spiritual implications? (Penny)*

R   I'm not sure, Penny, which is the more intriguing – the question or the questioner! First let me commend your honesty, and say that I am far happier conducting the funeral of a professed non-believer than a church wedding of a couple who have no intention of giving any place or time to religious commitment in their lives together. But that doesn't answer the question!

You say you don't 'really' believe in God. It sounds as if you are not quite the non-believer you make yourself out to be. Also, why worry about the spiritual implications if you don't believe? If you are right, they won't apply! I believe you are like many good, honest, moral people who find faith difficult for many understandable reasons.

I would therefore be more than willing to conduct your funeral service (if you go before me), and commend you lovingly and hopefully to the mercy and grace of the God who loves you whatever your level of belief. But again, if you choose, I would help you towards a humanist who conducts secular funerals, consisting of music, poetry, and an appropriate sharing of the memories and hopes of the deceased person's life, within a ceremony in which the body is committed to the ground or to the fire in a reverent manner.

If you choose such for yourself, I think it would be well for you to talk it over with your loved ones first, so that they become used to the idea. Although there is a legitimate and respectable humanist society which will be altogether helpful to you, such funerals are still fairly rare, and many people might find it upsetting for there to be no prayers, no reading of Scripture and no reference to God or hope of life in him.

I would say that if my non-Christian loved ones or friends had not specifically stated that they desired a humanist funeral, I would give them a Christian service. But if they had made it clear that they did not want such a service, I would abide by their wishes.

I do think, though, that you should be careful in planning such a secular ceremony. One such humanist said that, in a ceremony he had conducted, a family included the Monty Python song, 'Always look on the bright side of life'. That sounds humorous outside the situation, but in the face of death and genuine grief, I think it sounds tasteless and vacuous. And in another such funeral, 'Some day over the rainbow' sounded to me simply trite and sentimental.

Of course, many trite, sentimental and stupid things are sung, said and prayed at so-called Christian funerals, and I have been present at funerals where, on the one hand, the deceased person has been eulogized out of all recognition, and where, on the other hand, the service has been so cold, boring and unfeeling that I have almost wept for the mourners in the face of a rigidly professional clergyman – women are better!

It seems to me that many non-believers are looking for a humane and warm ceremony of thanks and remembrance in which, though there is no specific religious element, there is also a reverent laying to rest of the loved one's remains in an appropriate manner. In such an atmosphere, people can grieve, express gratitude, and feel that they have participated in a 'rite of passage' which has a spiritual (though not a religious) dimension.

And about the spiritual implications. Well, religious ritual is not the basis of our acceptance by God! There have been people who have had all the ritual and ceremony that the Church can provide, but this does not detract from the fact that their lives may have been selfish, arrogant and oppressive to those under their authority. On the other hand, there have been those who have been blasted to death in war, or resigned to a pauper's grave, but have entered the kingdom of God with love and a joyful welcome. I would not pronounce final sentence upon any man or woman. If they have chosen a secular funeral out of honest motivations or because of a hypocritical or abusing Church, then they may well hear the welcome of a loving Saviour-God at the end of their earthly journey.

When I conducted my parents' funerals within three weeks of each other, it was a tearful, moving and yet loving experience for my sister and our whole family and friends. And when only two months ago I made a special journey from my hermitage to conduct the funeral of my Aunt Molly, within the reverent, liturgical service of the Anglican rite, I preached a homily which brought smiles and even gentle laughter to the grieving family and friends – because that was what Molly was like! And this was appreciated.

I think I have said enough to enable enquirers to move forward with an honest mind and heart. But don't put a Christian funeral out of your plans – for perhaps God *is*, and if he *is*, then he certainly loves you!

Reflection

If you are unsure about your beliefs, you should think about the funeral of loved ones (and your own), so why not obtain a copy of the humanist secular funeral ceremony, and then look at your parish church's funeral service. The very consideration of the two forms of this rite of passage may lead you to a further reflection on the meaning of life and death, and perhaps to the discovery of a spiritual dimension you never thought you possessed.

59

Stupid Christians

Q *Why do Christians claim responsibility for their own faults and flagellate themselves about them, while alienating all their own goodness and attributing it to God? Isn't this sick, depraved and disgusting? (Roland)*

R The use of abusive language and the belligerence in the question causes me to say: 'Ah, Roland is sounding off again, tongue in cheek. He's grimacing at the pomposity, pseudo-piety and po-faced earnestness of religious people.' I don't believe that you are genuinely angry, so I'll not take that path with you. I intend to jump to the defence of Christian belief and practice, but first let me acknowledge the truth in your accusation.

Yes, there are some Christians who seem to say that everything good, true and holy about them is due only and wholly to the grace of God, while all that is sinful, mucky, deviant and diseased is due to their corrupted and fallen human nature, deserving punitive action (flagellation or constant guilt-ridden confession).

Of course, there are some non-Christians who indulge in double-think too. They pride themselves that their good health, ebullient personality, fat bank balance and increasing goods and chattels are entirely due to their alert and clever mind, enterprising market sense, healthy genes and social versatility. And their poor health, deviant practices, immoral earnings and broken relationships are due to other people's stupidity, lack of business acumen, antagonistic perversity or deprived childhood.

I don't excuse either category: both of them are not only subjective in their evaluations, but morally undiscerning. Therefore they are immature at best, and living in a kind of unreal world in which they will, sooner or later, be tripped up and made to face themselves honestly. They will discover the truth that they are better (in some ways) and worse (in others) than they thought themselves to be.

I must admit that there are times when it is a great temptation to affirm in Harriet Auber's beautiful, but sentimental, lines:

> Every virtue we possess,
> And every victory won,
> And every thought of holiness
> Are His alone.[1]

It sounds very pious, and I've often sung and meant it. But to be honest it is neither good theology or good psychology. The truth is that I'm much of a mixture. I have a certain natural gentleness, sensitivity, genuine love and concern for people, and natural gifts of communication, with a sunny and humorous temperament which (some) people find attractive. Why pretend otherwise? But it is also true that I am secretly conceited, like helping people who are winsome and attractive, and I have not always been sympathetic towards other people's moral and intellectual slips – especially when they are cleverer or more personable than I am!

It takes quite a bit of maturity and a real sense of discernment to sort out what kind of character I really am, and whether I am growing in wisdom or continuing to project an acceptable and laudable image.

That is why I need the grace and mercy of God for my real sins and stupidities. Then I need the honest fellowship of friends (and enemies). The Celtic soul friend is only genuine if he or she *burns* you with frank criticism and counsel. A bad book review makes me realize that I'm not as indifferent to the opinion of others as I had thought!

I suppose that I'm saying, yes, we are *all* sick, depraved and disgusting – but also that we are not so bad! We are all caught up in the human situation in which there are rarely the stark contrasts of black and white, but more often shades of grey. This applies to people and nations.

Whether my pilgrimage is a religious one on the road to sanctification, or a humanist one on the Jungian road to individuation, I must not expect counsels of perfection. Earnestly to practise perfection is a burden to oneself and a pain in the neck to others. To profess to have attained it is unbearable in both directions.

I would encourage you to continue the individuation process – it might make you a bit more tolerant of us hypocritical (but not too unlikeable) Christians, and if I follow Christ a bit more closely, that will make me more sympathetic, more warm-hearted – and more human!

Reflection

Christians and humanists have their own particular hypocrisies. Let me be aware of mine, and laugh at the ridiculousness of it all. In this way I shall become a little more humble, a little more simple, and a lot more loving!

60

The Cost of Forgiving Love

Q *Christians claim that Jesus died for our sins. Why couldn't God just forgive us – did Jesus need to die? (Gina)*

R Your question sounds like a simple and straightforward one, Gina, and the answer could be: 'Yes, God could have simply forgiven us because he desired to'. But there is more to it than that – much more.

First of all, if God had acted towards us as a judge pronouncing our forgiveness, we would not have valued such forgiveness or understood what the whole weight and burden of human sin meant to him – for a judge is concerned with justice, equity, ransom and balance. Or even if God had spoken our forgiveness as a good parent, we would not have truly seen the grief and sorrow by which our sins pierced his heart of love, and forgiveness would have been cheap to us. We would have got off scot-free, with no recompense or realization of the depth and gravity of sin. After all, we are not speaking just of plain acts of thoughtlessness or selfishness to which we are all prone, but of such personal sins as the calculating cruelty of the older bully who victimizes younger children;

141

the abuser who sexually attacks and even kills an innocent child; the violent man who beats wife and children month after month, year after year, reducing them to cringing fear.

If we turn to the corporate sin of the twentieth century, there springs immediately to mind the Holocaust in which six million Jews were butchered, gassed and burnt by an evil dictator and his vicious Nazi regime – or the many millions of Soviet people tortured and murdered by atheistic Communism under Stalin.

For God to grant forgiveness, there not only has to be profound and heartfelt repentance on the part of the offender, but God must show his loving and righteous anger against sin. He must so identify himself in love with our poor sinful race that it becomes fearfully and horribly clear that our sins have crucified our God, and that God himself becomes incarnate to bear, carry and exhaust the whole weight and burden of our sins against one another, which in reality are against him.

When I say God 'must', I don't mean that there is any law that compels him, but that his own loving, righteous and compassionate nature drives him, for love's sake, to take upon himself forgiving love, and to allow human wickedness to throw against him all that it can. All this he accepted lovingly, tenderly, non-violently, and cried out, even when we nailed him to the cross: 'Forgive them, for they know not what they do'.

You see, forgiveness is costly. A woman cannot lightly say to a terrorist murderer (of either side) in Northern Ireland: 'I forgive you for killing my son'. Nor can parents easily say to the couple in Gloucester who calculatingly over the years enticed, sexually abused, raped, murdered and buried many girl victims: 'For all that . . . we forgive you'. There must be tears and sweat and blood . . . there must be some kind of atonement, retribution, justice, reparation; there must be sorrow, repentance, penance, payment.

Now let me make this clear. I am *not* proposing lynching, flogging, hanging, execution – far from it. I am talking about the victim taking upon himself the whole weight and burden of sin's terror and torture, and bearing it away into the hell of grief and tears, abandoned dereliction, loneliness, alienation and death. And God did all that for us!

Out of the many Scriptures which strive to portray the meaning of the cross there is this beautiful text: 'In Christ God was reconciling the world to himself, not counting their trespasses against them, and entrusting the message of reconciliation to us' (2 Corinthians 5.19).

In Old Testament days it was thought that, in some mysterious way, the high priest could transfer the sins of the people to the scapegoat and then drive it out into the wilderness of desolation to die; or that he could lay the sins upon a sacrificial lamb so that its blood could somehow atone for sin. Such blood sacrifices could never cleanse away sin (Hebrews 10.4); but when John the Baptist bore witness to Jesus, he said: 'Here is the Lamb of God who takes away the sin of the world' (John 1.29). Christ is the fulfilment of all the types and yearnings of Old Testament piety, for it is by his reconciling work that God showed the depth of his love and the extent of his mercy to us.

The top of the cross reaches right into the tender heart of God; the base of the cross reaches down to the lowest depth of hell to which humankind could ever sink; the arms of the cross reach out to all people everywhere. God, incarnate in Christ, dies upon the cross, and because he is God, rises from death's power and penalty to become our risen Saviour and Lord. One of the loveliest prayers at the Eucharist puts it like this:

He opened wide his arms for us on the cross;
he put an end to death by dying for us
and revealed the resurrection by rising to new life.[1]

There is a great deal more to it, and the next chapter will reveal a different aspect to the cross. But although God could have received our repentance and faith, and forgiven us outright and simply, he desired to show us how much our sin cost him, and how much he tenderly loves us - even to the end. So look upon that cross and be filled with tears, with love and with joy.

Reflection
Spend some time before a cross, crucifix or an icon of the crucifixion. Read through the hymn, 'When I survey the wondrous cross', and ask God to help you make that hymn your prayer.

61

The Symbol of the Cross

Q *How can I understand the symbolic meaning of the cross? It is so ugly to think of it as an instrument of death.* (Peder)

R It is amazing, Peder, that the sign of our redemption and the means of our life should be a Roman gibbet – the instrument of execution. No wonder it was not the immediate symbol that early Christians used to signify their faith. The sign of the fish seems to have been their favoured one, for the Greek word for fish is *ixthus*, and it could be used as an acrostic:

I = Iesous (Jesus)
X = Christos (Christ)
Th = Theou (God's)
U = Huios (Son)
S = Sotēr (Saviour)

The sign is found in the catacombs, and it is said that it could easily be traced by a foot on the sand or dust as a secret faith-sign between believers during persecution.

As Christians increasingly understood that the bitter cross meant sweetest healing, prayers and hymns were composed which reflected this symbolism, like the beautiful words of Bishop Venantius Fortunatus (born 530):

> Faithful Cross! above all other
> One and only noble tree!
> None in foliage, none in blossom,
> None in fruit thy peer may be;
> Sweetest wood and sweetest iron!
> Sweetest weight was laid on thee.[1]

And in the Preface for the Cross at the Eucharist we read: 'The tree of shame was made the tree of glory; and where life was lost, there life has been restored'.[2]

I recently read a comment by a sympathetic Buddhist that he did not understand why the sign of the Christian faith was a crucified man in the agony of death, while the symbol of Buddhism was the meditating Buddha, lifted above the sorrowful and changing world. Well, I believe there is a complementarity in these two symbols; but before I can appreciate the tranquillity of the meditating Buddha, I need to know that the One through whom all things were made, became incarnate and entered into the agony and suffering of the cross for my redemption. I can sink to no depth that he has not plumbed before me, and know no suffering that he does not understand.

In my hermitage, above the altar-table, I have a large mounted reproduction of the San Damiano crucifix which spoke to St Francis in the early twelfth century. It is not a Western crucifixion of agony, but has a Byzantine ethos – the face of Christ is tender and compassionate, and painted around the cross are 27 smaller figures. Immediately above the head of the crucified Christ is the risen Christ facing ten disciples in glory (Judas is missing). Immediately at the right (wounded) side of Christ are Mary, his mother, and the disciple John. On the other side are Mary Magdalene and Mary the wife of Clopas, and the centurion with two soldiers. Above them, either side of the outstretched arms, are six angels, and below his feet are two dim figures which may be Adam and Eve or two Old Testament saints.

The beauty of all this is that the crucified Christ is also the risen Christ, for his arms are outstretched to save, and the whole company of the redeemed surround the cross, with the angelic company – representing the communion of saints in glory.

This is how the cross is to be understood, not as an instrument of torture and execution, but as the tree of life, and the thorn-crowned Saviour is the King of Glory reigning from his throne.

One of the loveliest crucifixes, which I lived with for five years, is the large *Christus Rex* figure over the side altar at St Mary's Episcopal Cathedral, Glasgow. The Christ is robed as priest and king, and although he is lifted up on the cross, he is at the same time triumphant and the reigning one. This, and the San Damiano crucifix, remind us of the One who said: 'Do not be afraid; I am the living One. I was dead, and see, I am alive forever and ever; and have the keys of Death and of Hades' (Revelation 1.17–18).

145

Reflection

Take your church hymn book and turn to the section on the cross and passion of Christ. Go through some of the hymns over the next few days and see the way in which the cross of shame becomes the tree of glory – so let your life be transformed.

Epilogue

A THEOLOGIAN IS ONE WHO PRAYS

This book contains a small selection of the questions with which I have been bombarded over the years – from my young days as a Christian working in the commercial and hospital spheres, then as a theological student, a working pastor and priest, a university chaplain, a peripatetic Franciscan friar and, over the last eight years, in exploring the hermit life.

One part of me has always enjoyed theological discussion, human enquiry and apologetic dialogue. I have always been energized by the cut-and-thrust of debate, especially with those with whom I disagree in the warmth of controversy, but not in the negative heat of mere argument.

This book is somewhat different. I have not reproduced the dialogue and correspondence which still passes between myself and other friends (Christian and non-Christian), for much of this is long, involved, and often demands theological training.

Evagrius, the desert monk, said that one who prays is a theologian, and a theologian is one who prays – and that has been the spirit of this book. The questions all came as a result of the Questionnaire, and I have responded to, though not always 'answered', the questions. I have soaked the book in prayer and thought, and much of its response has been formulated while digging, bookbinding or walking through the fields with Mungo the monastery dog, as well as upon my knees in my chapel hut.

Although all the responses have come from me, they emerge from decades of thought and prayer, shared in the communion of saints, and in the ministry and fellowship of sisters and brothers in Christ. I have sought not to be denominational or exclusive, though it is clear that I am not vague in my understanding of the way of Christ.

I do not impose the demands and insights of my own particular path upon anyone else's life, nor do I urge people to sell up their homes, leave their families and embark on a hermit life in a wooden hut! Rather, I have sought to share something of the joy, the insights, the spirituality and the enlightenment of my pilgrimage with the readers, so that they may incorporate such principles into their own thinking and living.

The opening quotation from Alessandro Pronzato comes from a book which I share with all the novices who 'do their time' at Glasshampton monastery, in whose grounds my hermitage stands. This particular quotation has guided my prayer and thinking, for like Alessandro, all my perplexing questions fall into mute wonder and silence before the mystery of God.

Yet I have not lost my questions – indeed, they increase as time goes by – but they become relative and part of the whole human quest and pilgrimage, and I fall back upon the words of St Paul:

> I consider that the sufferings of this present time are not worthy to be compared with the glory about to be revealed to us . . . For we know that all things work together for good to those who love God, who are called according to his purpose (Romans 8.18, 28).

The questions and responses gathered in this book are to encourage the reader to the greater quest, adventure and pilgrimage of love. This includes deepening your life of contemplative prayer, developing a profounder relationship of compassion with your friends and enemies, and living a positive life of joy among the troubles and hopes of our world.

If Christ radiates from your life, and if this world is a better place for your having lived, then when our Lord returns in glory, we shall have reason to continue with him in gratitude and joy into that eternal pilgrimage of love.

References

Preliminary pages
Alessandro Pronzato (1982), *Meditations on the Sand*, St Paul Publications, p. 92.

1 IS CHRISTIANITY THE ONLY WAY?

1 From C. F. Alexander, 'Once, in royal David's city', in *The New English Hymnal* (1986), The Canterbury Press.
2 From Charles Wesley, 'Hark! the herald angels sing', in *The New English Hymnal* (1986), The Canterbury Press.

3 THEOLOGICAL TRAINING – HERESY AND DEVOTION

1 Simone Weil (1951), *Waiting on God*, Routledge & Kegan Paul, p. 22.

4 INFALLIBILITY?

1 Hans Küng (1968), *The Church*, Search Press; (1971) *Infallibility* (Collins).
2 St Vincent of Lerins, *Commonitorium* XXIII, 28.
3 Quoted in Archimandrite Sophrony (1991), *Saint Silouan the Athonite* (Monastery of St John the Baptist), pp. 87f.
4 St Augustine, untraced.

5 UNDERSTANDING THE TRINITY

1 John Macquarrie, 'Understanding the Trinity' (revised edition 1977), *The Principles of Christian Theology*, SCM, pp. 90–202.

6 OFFER OF SALVATION AFTER DEATH?

1 Ramon SSF (to be published during 1998), *The Prayer Mountain*, The Canterbury Press.
2 The Doctrine Commission of the Church of England (1995), *The Mystery of Salvation*, Church House Publishing.

8 GOD FEELING TIRED?

1 John Macquarrie (1997), *Principles of Christian Theology*, SCM.
2 Alister McGrath (1994), *Christian Theology*, Blackwell; (1995), *The Christian Theology Reader*, Blackwell.

9 SPIRITUALITY – WHAT DOES IT MEAN?

1 Gordon Wakefield (1983), *A Dictionary of Christian Spirituality*, SCM, p. 362.
2 Thomas Merton (1953), *The Sign of Jonas*, Burns & Oates.
3 See Note 1.

11 WHY ALL THE SIN AND MISERY?

1 Ramon SSF (1988), *Fulness of Joy*, Marshall Pickering, p. 6.

12 CREATION AND REDEMPTION

1 Ramon SSF (1988), *Fulness of Joy*, Marshall Pickering, pp. 17–18.

13 INTELLECT, EMOTION AND INTUITION

1 *The New Jerome Biblical Commentary* (1991), Geoffrey Chapman.
2 Raymond E. Brown (1997), *An Introduction to the New Testament*, Doubleday.
3 Michael Mayne (1995), *This Sunrise of Wonder*, HarperCollins.
4 Hans Küng (1970), *The Christian Challenge*, Collins.

17 NODDING OFF IN PRAYER

1 The Daily Office SSF (1992), Mowbray. A version of the SSF office book is now generally available under the title *Celebrating Common Prayer* (1992), Mowbray.

19 SCARED OF A MONASTERY?

1 Ramon SSF (1987), *Deeper into God*, Marshall Pickering.
2 Andrew Nash (1997), *The Vision*, The National Retreat Association, p. 13.

20 GRACE AND CONTEMPLATION

1 Michael Saward (1997), *The Post-Evangelical Debate*, SPCK, p. 86.
2 Olivier Clément (1993), *The Roots of Christian Mysticism*, New City.

21 CONTEMPLATIVE PRAYER TODAY

1 William Johnston (1995), *Mystical Theology*, HarperCollins.
2 Christopher Bryant (1987), *Depth Psychology and Religious Belief*, Darton, Longman & Todd.
3 Kallistos Ware (1979), *The Orthodox Way*, Mowbray.
4 Michael Mitton (1995), *Restoring the Woven Cord*, Darton, Longman & Todd.
5 David Adam (1988), *The Cry of the Deer*, SPCK.
6 Anthony de Mello (1984), *Sadhana*, Image Books.
7 John Main (1998), *Silence and Stillness in Every Season*, ed. Paul Harris, Darton, Longman & Todd.

22 MANY ROUTES TO GOD?

1 Ramon SSF (1989), *Soul Friend*, Marshall Pickering.
2 Thomas Merton (1965), *The Way of Chuang Tzu*, New Directions.

23 LEARNING FROM WORLD FAITHS

1 See Documents of Vatican II, quoted in Thomas Merton (1966), *Mystics and Zen Masters*, Dell Publishing.
2 Thomas Merton (1966), *Mystics and Zen Masters*, Dell Publishing.

25 BUDDHIST–CHRISTIAN FRIENDSHIP

1 Bede Griffiths (1989), *A New Vision of Reality*, Collins, p. 273.
2 In Thomas Merton (1963), *Faith and Violence*, University of Notre Dame, pp. 106ff.

3 A. M. Allchin (ed.) (1989), *Heart of Compassion; Readings with St Isaac of Syria*, Darton, Longman & Todd.

27 JAZZ AND QUAKER SILENCE

1 Jan Garbarek/The Hilliard Ensemble (1993), *Officium*, cassette ECM 1525.
2 Duke Ellington (1974), *Sacred Concert*, Prestige CD, PCD-24045-2.
3 George Steiner (1989), *Real Presences*, Faber & Faber.

32 GOD IN THE PRESENT MOMENT

1 Brother Lawrence, *The Practice of the Presence of God*.
2 *The Legend of Perugia*, 80.

37 ORGAN TRANSPLANTS – GIFT OR PRESUMPTION?

1 Morris West (1990), *Lazarus*, Heinemann, p. 7.

39 DIFFICULT TO FORGIVE

1 Michael Mitton and Russ Parker (1991), *Requiem Healing*, Daybreak.

41 GOING GREEN

1 Peter Selby (1997), *Grace and Mortgage*, Darton, Longman & Todd.

42 CHRISTIANS, BUDDHISTS AND ATHEISTS TOGETHER

1 Hans Küng (1991), *Global Responsibility: In Search of a New World Ethic*, SCM.
2 Ramon SSF (1994), *Franciscan Spirituality: Following Saint Francis Today*, SPCK.

45 A DOCTOR'S DILEMMA

1 Elisabeth Kübler-Ross (1970), *On Death and Dying*, Tavistock Publications.

49 STICK-AND-CARROT THEOLOGY

1 John Whittier, 'Immortal Love for ever full', in *The New English*

Hymnal (1986), The Canterbury Press.

2 From *Studies in the Spanish Mystics*.

55 BRITAIN A CHRISTIAN COUNTRY?

1 Thomas Merton (1970), *The Wisdom of the Desert*, New Directions.
2 Quoted in Eric Hobsbawm (1955), *Age of Extremes*, Michael Joseph, p. 558.

57 INEQUALITIES, INJUSTICE, IMBALANCE

1 Harold S. Kushner (1987), *When Bad Things Happen to Good People*, Pan Books.

59 STUPID CHRISTIANS

1 Harriet Auber, 'Our Blest Redeemer', in *The English Hymnal* (1933), Oxford University Press.

60 THE COST OF FORGIVING LOVE

1 From the Third Eucharistic Prayer, Alternative Service Book 1980, SPCK, p. 136.

61 THE SYMBOL OF THE CROSS

1 Bishop Venantius Fortunatus, in *The New English Hymnal* (1986), The Canterbury Press.
2 Proper Preface 9, Alternative Service Book 1980, SPCK, p. 155.

Useful Addresses

1 The National Retreat Association, The Central Hall,
256 Bermondsey Street, London SE1 3UJ.

2 The World Community for Christian Meditation (John Main
OSB). The Christian Meditation Centre, 29 Campden Hill,
London W8 7DX.

3 Green Christians – *The Christian Ecology Link* (CEL),
20 Carlton Road, Harrogate, North Yorkshire HG2 8DD.

4 The Church Commissioners, 1 Millbank, London SW1P 3JZ.

5 The Bible Reading Fellowship, Peter's Way, Sandy Lane West,
Oxford OX4 5HG.

6 The Scripture Union, 207–209 Queensway, Bletchley,
Milton Keynes MK2 2EB.

The Society for Promoting Christian Knowledge (SPCK) was founded in 1698. It has as its purpose three main tasks:

- **Communicating the Christian faith in its rich diversity**

- **Helping people to understand the Christian faith and to develop their personal faith**

- **Equipping Christians for mission and ministry**

SPCK Worldwide serves the Church through Christian literature and communication projects in over 100 countries. Special schemes also provide books for those training for ministry in many parts of the developing world. SPCK Worldwide's ministry involves Churches of many traditions. This worldwide service depends upon the generosity of others and all gifts are spent wholly on ministry programmes, without deductions.

SPCK Bookshops support the life of the Christian community by making available a full range of Christian literature and other resources, and by providing support to bookstalls and book agents throughout the UK. SPCK Bookshops' mail order department meets the needs of overseas customers and those unable to have access to local bookshops.

SPCK Publishing produces Christian books and resources, covering a wide range of inspirational, pastoral, practical and academic subjects. Authors are drawn from many different Christian traditions, and publications aim to meet the needs of a wide variety of readers in the UK and throughout the world.

The Society does not necessarily endorse the individual views contained in its publications, but hopes they stimulate readers to think about and further develop their Christian faith.

For further information about the Society, please write to:
SPCK, Holy Trinity Church, Marylebone Road,
London NW1 4DU, United Kingdom.